Songs of Three Islands

Atlas & Co.
New York

Songs of Three Islands

A Story of Mental Illness in an Iconic American Family

Millicent Monks

Grateful acknowledgement to: "Accused Doctor Suspended,"
Copyright 1990, Globe Newspaper Company, on pages 126–27,
republished with permission; James S. Rockefeller for the letter quoted
on page 12; *Medical News Today* for the article reprinted in Appendix I.

Atlas & Co. *Publishers*
15 West 26th Street, 2nd floor
New York, NY 10010
www.atlasandco.com

Distributed to the trade by W. W. Norton & Company

Printed in the United States

Atlas & Company books may be purchased for educational, business,
or sales promotional use. For information, please write to
info@atlasandco.com.

Library of Congress Cataloging-in-Publication Data is available upon
request.

ISBN: 978-1-934633-34-2
14 13 12 11 10   1 2 3 4 5 6

To Bobby

All my life, until old age dulled my dreams, I felt like a metaphor, struggling to grow a skin. By the time of my sixtieth birthday, the skin finally crept around my edges, scabby at first and hard, but eventually it softened, leaving only a small scar.

It was then that I understood that I was loved, through the long, patient, loving care that my husband had bestowed upon me all these years.

In some ways acquiring a skin is very confining, because one is forced into bodily form and cannot move and dance through the connectedness of things so easily. Perhaps being a metaphor, though terrifying at times, brings one closer to the spirit.

Only love made the skin bearable; otherwise, the longing for the other side would have become too powerful. One might not remain here.

Foreword

In the years when I was writing this book, people would ask me what I did and I would say, "I am writing a book about mental illness in my family." Again and again, to my surprise, people would tell me about the mental illness and the pain in their families as if it were a great relief to talk about it—some were people I had known for years, and I had previously had no idea what they had been through. Some sent long letters.

They shared so many sad and terrible tales, often describing how they dealt with mental illness, as best they could. Some shared tales of love and anger—and of heroic lives in the face of tragedy and loss.

As I grew older I found the life of the spirit (not religion) became a place of silence and light that helped me through the tragic destructiveness of serious mental illness in my family, and helped me to keep loving those affected, even though it was to affect my health and my ability to be all I had hoped to have been.

My greatest wish for this book is that it may help mental illness come out of the dark ages and shed a bit of light on it. I hope that for some it might be an experience shared by all of us who suffer from what we don't understand—and in that way be healing.

My marriage brought together these three islands on the East Coast. This is the story of those islands, their heritage and of three women and a child. It is of Lucy, the grandmother; her daughter, me, Millicent; Sandra, my daughter; and her daughter, Sidra (the great granddaughter). It is a story of serious mental illness, wounding, destruction, despair, healing and love set against the background of these islands, and the story shows the sometimes devastating effects on my life and that of my husband.

Lucy carried within her the jungle and the spirit of the south. Sandra has also leaned towards the southern island. My granddaughter, Sidra, will choose her island in due time.

But I, Millicent, am northern born and drawn to the north wind – the cold wind of crystals and white snow which covers every living thing with a softness that burns and freezes so no human thing can function, so that the soul must fly out and nestle in the chasm of the north wind's lair, where it rests curled in the silence, emptiness and comfort, where time took on a different significance – circular, not linear, spiritual and eternal. Behind the kingdom of the north wind lives death. So entwined am I with this nature that barely a day goes by that I have not thought of death or rubbed against her knowingly, but that is the way of the north wind, and I cannot help it. We have had a battle, she and I. Some pedantic souls call it fantasy, but I call her the north wind, and she has whispered her message in my ears for a long time now, and I know of burning ice and crystals, and a land where there are no limits, and where images are cracked and deadly and melt together under the ice. How I have loved and feared her. In my mind she became my mother.

North Wind

Part One

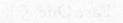

Cumberland Island

To the Deep South there is an island, female in spirit and ruled by a matriarchy. It is called Cumberland Island. Hot, lush, sensuous with wild and crawling animals, the curved lines of the banyan trees, cozy with death and fertile with life, the jungle, primeval and seductive, devouring—this was my mother's island. She was Lucy Coleman Carnegie, named after her grandmother. There the soft light was wet and heavy with moisture. The jungle claimed my mother and sang to her of its primitive childlike nature, and of its poisons, which would claim her.

My mother, Lucy Carnegie, was born in 1904, and grew up on a southern island, Cumberland Island, off the coast of Florida, an island that might have broken from some mythical land and drifted on ancient tides till it settled among the marshes and sloughs in the Deep South. Twenty-five miles of beach, edged by carved and billowing dunes (twenty to forty feet high), ending to the north at a long stone jetty filled with oysters and crabs, and to the south by marshes and creeks where sharks swam up in the spring to give birth and foolish young cousins swam in its warm waters.

Rattlers thick as arms wound themselves like vines around the live oak and slithered down trunks to lie across the white crushed-oyster-shell roads to enjoy the sun. Alligators filled the swamps and wild boar with curved tusks snorted and stomped through the palmettos. Wild turkeys spread their tail feathers and wild horses roamed in herds across the fields and beach and into the dunes.

Like all islands it was a place that generated its own peculiar brand of excitement, its own closed community, scandals, way of life, and its own morality and laws—instant justice. The island floated away from the real world with its uncanny beauty, riches, and wilderness; its gray hanging Spanish moss that crept through the trees at night and strangled them. In the spring, great, powerful sea turtles, about three feet long, laid their ping-pong eggs in the sand and buried them with their back flippers, and then were ridden back to the sea by the children, leaving their eggs to be rooted out and eaten by wild boar. The island held in its winding circumference all that was exotic, wanton, irreligious and excitingly feminine. It was teeming with life and sudden death and it was hell-bent on enticement.

The island was bought by Lucy's grandfather, Thomas Carnegie, for his wife, Lucy Coleman, and their nine children, in the 1870s, from General William Mackay Davis after the Civil War, under rather ominous circumstances. The general had just finished redoing Dungeness, his large mansion, adding a tower to the main house and quarters for the help. Except for the Stafford Plantation twelve miles down the island, it was the only other plantation.

One late afternoon Mrs. Davis called her husband to the veranda and asked him to shoot some of the birds in the big banyan trees close to the house, so she could have the cook make a stew for dinner. General Davis took his gun and shot and killed his own five-year-old son, mistaking him in the branches for a bird. The newspaper recorded the incident.

As my aunt recorded it, right after the child fell General Davis said,

*"My darling, did Papa shoot you?" The boy said, "Yes,
Papa." Mr. Davis hastened to the child and noticed a red
stain on his lip and asked, "Did Papa shoot you in the
mouth?" "No Papa, right here," he answered, putting
his left hand on the wound over his right arm and side.
He looked up beseechingly at his father but without outcry
or screaming. Mr. Davis took him up and, as he did so,
a violent hemorrhage came from the child's lips and in
less than fifteen minutes the little fellow was beyond the
pass of shadows.*

*It spread a cloud of horror over our little com-
munity, and all tender to the bereaved parents their
heartfelt sympathy. It is needless to add that the parents are almost crazed by this terrible, heartrending
disaster.*

The general's misery was such that after the incident he
sold the island to Thomas with the only stipulation being
that he be allowed back once a year to visit his son's grave.
He never came back. It was to be the island John F. Kennedy,
Jr. was married on.

"Thomas Carnegie, born in Dunfermline, Scotland, in
September 1843, of humble but educated parentage, arrived
in America poverty stricken," wrote my aunt, Nancy Carnegie
Rockefeller, in a self-published memoir, *The Carnegies &
Cumberland Island*. "The little family consisted of two
sons, Thomas and Andrew." The brothers worked hard and
were connected to the Scottish community of Pittsburgh.
Thomas joined his older brother Andrew Carnegie in the
steel business and became immensely wealthy. Eventually
he married a wealthy young lady, Lucy Coleman, of Irish
background. In 1860 he went into business with a Mr. Henry
Phipps, Jr. "He was known as a modest and unassuming man,
a family man without an enemy in the world," according to
my aunt. "When he bought the island it included an estate

and large house known as Dungeness. He added on to the grounds of the old plantation and to Dungeness until it became a castle of European grandeur that grew out of the sandy soil of the jungle on the end of an isolated island."

Its grim name spread its roots into the earth and grew up in rich, dark wood, stone, and marble. Dungeness: with its tower looking far out over the salt marshes and ocean, its large high-ceilinged rooms with fireplaces shining with brass and smooth carved wood, its big wraparound terrace with wooden swings, where tea was brought in a silver service in the late afternoons, and long low steps were guarded by huge potted plants that stretched out to the fountains in the gardens. Crystal, silks, monogrammed, handmade silver brushes and combs, and delicate rose-patterned china were rewards for arriving out of terrible poverty—a poverty soon forgotten.

Thomas planted gardens, olive groves, and lemon and orange trees around his plantation. He built a school for his nine children, a small railroad from the dock to Dungeness, stables for horses and carriages, a dairy for some forty cows, large sheds for chickens and hogs, tabby houses made of equal parts lime, water, sand, oyster shells, and ash to bake in, and one to do the daily laundry, another to store candles and space for the seamstresses, a house for the doctor and nurse, an infirmary, a house for carpentry, a large three-story house for the white help, and quarters for the blacks. There were tennis courts and a golf course. It was said that eventually it took three hundred servants to run the Dungeness estate and other estates that were soon built. An enormous wooden building a short way from the main house held several squash courts, a gym, a billiard room, and a long, cool, green pool with a set of rings on which one could swing across the water.

Years later when I was young and living on the island one summer, before the building collapsed, I swung naked across the pool on those rings, sailing back and forth, arching through the warm, stale air until exhaustion made me drop into the slightly brackish, cool, sulfur-smelling water, laughing until it echoed too loudly through the empty rooms.

2

Lucy's Island

Thomas moved his nine children and his wife, Lucy Coleman (he later named one of the steel furnaces after her, as furnaces, like ships and women, were considered temperamental and dangerous), to the island in 1881, when it was still deserted. He lived on the island for about three years but was exhausted from the labor of building the Carnegie steel business with his brother, Andrew. In 1886, he caught pneumonia and died at the age of forty-two, leaving his wife with the deed to the island under her pillow, a mansion, and nine children. This was the beginning of the matriarchy of Cumberland Island, which continues to this day.

In my Aunt Nan's history of the island, she writes:

> One of Lucy's [or Mama Negie as she came to be known] objectives was her building program. She wanted to enlarge recreational facilities for her family. One old cotton field (Old House Field) became a skeet field. Stafford House Field became a golf course. New roads were cut to facilitate duck shooting or deer hunting. Other old roads became trails for pleasure riding.
>
> Five substantial houses were added to the estate (for the children) between 1893 and 1903: Plum Orchard; Greyfields; the Cottage; fixed up and enlarged an empty and dilapidated Stafford; and the Pool House next to Dungeness, facetiously called The Casino for the only two sons who remained bachelors and their friends.

Mama Negie bought several boats, including a seventy-five-foot steam yacht called the *Missoe*—probably because the Timucuan Indians who lived on the island as early as four thousand years ago called the island Missoe, which means "beautiful island"—and a 119-foot yacht called the *Dungeness*. She was the first woman member of the New York Yacht Club. She rode horseback with the children, played golf, shot with the boys, and in later years drove her own electric car. She often visited Uncle Andrew at Skibo, his castle in Scotland. After Thomas died, Andrew, who was still a bachelor, asked Mama Negie to marry him. She refused. She was thought to be indomitable. By 1908, she owned all of Cumberland except for two miles at the northern end and dominated the lives of everyone on the island. The family created a Brigadoon-like fantasy, which they could never leave because they couldn't function in the outside world; somehow it had slipped through their fingers.

As the nine children grew up, Mama Negie asked her third son, Andrew Carnegie II (my grandfather), and his wife, Bertha Sherlock, to stay on at Dungeness and help run the estate; they had two daughters, Lucy and Nan, which is how Lucy Carnegie, my mother, and her older sister, Nan, grew up in Dungeness at the height of its glory. It soon became clear that something wasn't quite right with Lucy.

Bertha helped with the household and arranged most of the activities: masquerades, tennis tournaments, croquet tournaments, picnics, beach parties, card games, plays, and endless gatherings for guests. The men spent their time shooting, fishing, digging for clams and oysters at the jetty, boating to other islands, and going on moonlight sails. My mother Lucy took part in plays and dressed in costumes from Paris. Evenings were spent listening to the elders read aloud or playing the piano and singing. There were picnics deep in the island under large oak trees and swimming in the warm night air on the beach.

Lucy's room at Dungeness, with its large windows reaching the floor, looked down over the back garden and fountain. Her first memories as a child as she fell asleep in the evening must have been the night sounds of tree frogs in chorus, the splashing of water in the fountain, the swishing and rustling of palm trees. An island lullaby. It was probably her last lullaby, for Lucy's life was not to be a happy one.

In the morning, she woke early to the braying of Sicilian mules that worked in the fields. When she was eight or so, if she arose early enough to escape her governess, she would pull on the special pants her grandmother had designed for her so she could ride astride and not sidesaddle. Lucy loved to ride. She would sneak down to the barn with its fifty horses and many carriages and talk the head groom into letting her ride in the field next to the barn. Then she'd return to a formal English breakfast placed on the sideboard with heaters. The table was decorated with beautiful flowers and laden with eggs, sausages, pancakes, and homemade breads and jams.

Lucy became an excellent rider and was proficient at training the wild island horses. Tabby, Lucy's cousin of the same age, also loved horses. Tabby looked like an Indian and carried a knife on her belt. Uncle Rasty, who was married to one of the Carnegie girls, organized the children's cavalry— Lucy was Captain Prickle Bush. They rode the wild horses at a gallop down the twenty-five-mile beach under the full moon, and through the palmettos and oak trees, rooting out wild turkeys and boars with fierce, white tusks.

In all of the pictures of Lucy as a child, she looks sad and angry, and her mouth turns sharply downward, probably a hint of what was to come. She never forgot anything that had bothered her, which was disconcerting. She clung to the belief that her mother and father "loved Nan more than her," my aunt recalled. Nan was a favorite with the girls' mother, Bertha; Lucy and Bertha never got along. Some of my cousins described Bertha as cold and distant. With her dark hair and blue eyes, she was said to be the most beautiful of the Sherlock girls. (They were Mama Negie's two sisters.) I think my grandparents really wanted a boy, as they had lost one. Lucy was a lovely girl with soft brown hair, blue eyes, and Scottish freckles, as well as a good, strong, athletic build and an Irish temperament—a bit on the wild side.

Lucy learned early on that people died of pneumonia, typhoid, riding accidents, and snake and spider bites. She knew that Uncle Bill's wife had died of typhoid and that after she was buried he dug her up, cut off her long blond braid, and wore it around his waist for years. She learned that being inquisitive could have frightening consequences when she snuck out of the house with Nan and her cousin Tom to see the boat that had washed up on the beach and had something to do with people called rumrunners. When the three of them got there, they found a red-haired dead man facedown in the sand with one arm eaten away by vultures.

She learned very young how to kill snakes and shoot deer. She was blooded by the time she was twelve—her face covered with the blood of the first deer she shot. She was there when word came that Stafford Plantation was on fire and the Sage Brush Cavalry galloped down to be part of the fire brigade, forming a long line to the marsh, filling buckets with water and passing them up the human line. She saw one of her aunts run into the burning house to save her "rat"—a piece of material used to put up ladies' hair. She learned that it wasn't so easy to put out a fire. Stafford Plantation burned to the ground.

There were always lots of people around—the grooms, the gardeners, the doctor and nurse, tennis and golf coaches, cousins, aunts, uncles, and visitors. Life was filled with excitement.

Lucy knew her father dispensed island justice when the black butler killed his wife's lover and came to Lucy's father, who after hearing the man's story, said, "Bury him then."

I believe today Lucy would be seen as an unstable or "troubled" child. She was impetuous and difficult and quick to anger. I think the island was good for Lucy: it contained her nature and gave her scope. Its wildness and dangers and constant drama satisfied her character. She was at one with its ghosts and spirits; the long, black nights lulled and comforted her. I think she loved the island more than she ever loved any human being.

When Uncle Andrew (Thomas's older brother, and therefore my mother's great-uncle) came to visit, which he did often, the children always wore their kilts and had to follow the butler around the table with the haggis (a Scottish dish made from sheep's pluck—heart, liver, and lungs—which smells terrible) on a silver tray. A bagpiper walking around the grounds woke them up in the morning and piped them into dinner. The gentlemen wore kilts and took the ladies' arms to escort them to the table. I remember this custom from when I stayed at Skibo Castle (Uncle Andrew's home in Scotland) with Aunt Nan many years later in the 1950s, visiting with Cousin Margaret, Andrew's daughter, and her children.

Lucy and Nan were very careful not to put sugar in their porridge when Uncle Andrew was there, ever since the day he rose up from the table at Skibo and announced, in front of the many guests, among whom were the English prime minister, Lord Morley, and Lord Shaw, "No Scottish lassie puts sugar on her porridge. Ne'er do it again." Aunt Nan later recalled that at this moment she prayed to make herself disappear. Family members also understood always to lose at cards when playing with Uncle Andrew; they even paid the children to do so.

When they were visiting Uncle Andrew at Skibo in 1914 at the beginning of World War I, they saw the Black Watch regiment, kilts swinging, march out of Edinburgh. "Ladies from Hell" the Germans called them. They nearly all died and Uncle Andrew was heartbroken after returning from the dedication of the Peace Palace at the Hague in Holland, and meeting with Kaiser William. When he learned that the Kaiser was not going to keep the peace, he kept saying, "How could Bill have done that to me?"

Dinner parties were a daily occurrence on Cumberland Island. The kitchen staff always prepared ten extra meals for last-minute guests. The huge oval table was set with a white tablecloth, silver candelabra, glasses with gold filigree, and plates rimmed with gold. A long rectangular mirror reflected the scene and the candlelight. The vegetables and flowers came from the large gardens. Chickens, eggs, milk, cream, turkey, venison, oysters, bread, and fish all came from the island. Everyone dressed up, ladies in full evening dress and men in tuxedos. Grandma Carnegie almost always wore a tiara, an egret feather, or a flower in her hair.

Without a man at the helm, the boys became undisciplined, except for my grandfather, who was of a quiet, gentle nature. He left college early to return to the island and run Dungeness, and always regretted not having a regular job or a decent education. The girls had little direction, living the American dream on a wild and glorious island amongst unheard-of riches. But some would become powerful women in the next generation and carry on the matriarchy.

In an unpublished memoir, my cousin, Pebble Rockefeller, wrote: "I came to realize that I was part of this tapestry woven by an incredible island and its endearing inhabitants. I came to appreciate the underlying sadness inherent in some of the Carnegie clan, exiled as they were to a remote island with a powerful matriarchal figure, leaving them nothing to do but hunt, fish, womanize, and drink too much and think what excitement was planned for the coming day. Some called the Carnegie women the great vulvacracy."

When Lucy was fifteen and Nan seventeen, Mama Negie got sick. She was known to disappear into the tower at Dungeness from time to time and not come down for meals. Sometimes she would go off crabbing by herself in a flat-bottom boat and fall asleep. Lucy and Nan's last memory of her was standing in front of the mirror in the large Dungeness hall adjusting her New York Yacht Club hat with a long hatpin, her hair and dress in disarray. She had been ill all winter. She looked down at them and said, "Girls, don't remember me like this." Mama Negie ended up in McLean, the famous hospital outside of Boston for those with mental problems. She died in 1916. Mama Negie's illness was never mentioned by my mother. You simply didn't talk about such things in those days.

Perhaps Lucy should never have left the island, but a couple of years later she saw her future husband, Sean, from the window of Charles Francis Adams's house on Commonwealth Avenue in Boston. Sean lived next door. He was tall and thin, with black hair, blue eyes, and a finely chiseled face. He was the captain of the Harvard polo team.

Aunt Nan wrote in her family book: "Sean was known to be a bit nutty. He drove cars too fast and was very spoiled. He sang cowboy songs and was full of the devil. He always walked on tiptoe and was never satisfied unless he was stirring things up. He was right down Lucy's alley. After his father died, no one could control him. He turned out to be not the father or husband he might have been."

Unfortunately, too, my father became a scatterer of seed amongst many ladies, an illness, I suppose, like kleptomania or alcoholism.

Lucy married him six months after she glimpsed him through the window, in a grand wedding at Dungeness. She was eighteen. A year later her sister Nan married J. Stillman Rockefeller at Dungeness.

The following letter fell out of my mother's album of

wedding pictures that I happened to open a few years ago. I checked with several "experts," one who had written a book about Carnegie, and was told it was an original. I have no idea how my mother got it (perhaps because her name was Lucy, the name of Carnegie's furnace #2).*

* See Appendix II for a transcription of this letter.

ANDREW CARNEGIE

New York May 8th - 76.

Messr. S M & H. P.

I cannot allow this foundation day of Second Furnace to pass unnoticed. It has given me the greatest satisfaction received from business for some years. We are now on the right road to bring our investments down to permanent value. — "Founded on the rock" we shall be, — Our course to a preeminent position among the Iron Manufrs of America — yes of the World — seems very clear to me. We need only to apply our profits to the development of our business, even undertaking an extension for which we have not the means —

I shall endeavor to restrain my natural tendency to go at a rapid pace. For

will agree to more as we earn the means
always however in developments or
improvements of the Am & Steel borders
& not outside thereof — And never let
us have notes out exceeding a small
sum per month — I agree to this
with all my heart — & am content to
make less rather than to give cause
for the least anxiety. Saying — "To be
thus is nothing, but to be safely thus".
We must remember however that we are
too young not to grow — & it is only a question
whether we concentrate, or scatter our
means — For my part I would have
the young Carnegies & Phipps weeded to
save great interest in which their pride
can be surely enlisted & to a vast
establishment which will necessarily
require their close attention — otherwise

New York

I could scarcely blame my nephews
were they to subside into No bodies
—or worse.—

The satisfaction I have in feeling that
our firm consists of you alone, is
unbounded.— How happily we are placed
& how well calculated to supplement
each other except that I always feel
my money is necessary to give me
equal part in the credit. as it is to
your services most is owing.

Three cheers for Lucy No 2.
& hurrah for O B & C.

Yours
The Senior.

3
Nuns

Sean and Lucy took their honeymoon in Europe and Africa, visiting friends and relatives, then returned to Crescent Island for the summer. They spent the winter in Boston.

In the beginning, Lucy enjoyed Sean's outrageousness. It made her feel less like an outcast in a world that wasn't her island, where human beasts could be cruel and her wild spirit had no home. She was pleased with his looks—strong, square, solid, and handsome, with a smile that let her in on a secret, that he was a naughty, powerful child who was going to eat all the cherries in the bowl. If she could keep up, life would be a great game filled with excitement. His overwhelming energy would sweep her up and give her a life full of drama. He would take responsibility for being wicked, and she wouldn't be condemned to a run-of-the-mill existence.

At first, Lucy was enchanted with the idea of being his wife and doing whatever he wished. She believed she wanted him to make all the decisions—she was still too young to know better—and he wanted it that way. He wanted a wife and a big family without any responsibility, certainly without the responsibility of a relationship.

One summer not long after they were married, they were visiting Lucy's relatives on the North Shore outside Boston. They were staying with a favorite cousin of Lucy's named Rita, one of the family's black sheep, who was attracted to too many men, often those considered socially unsuitable. After breakfast on the third day of their stay, Sean announced that he had to go to the city for several days on business. No one was surprised at his announcement, as he had inherited a large business from his father, although he never ran it himself. He treated his office like a private men's club that he darted in and out of from time to time, occasionally rearranging the furniture. He always said his genius was in hiring good people to run the business. He was highly intelligent, intuitive, and psychic, but he lacked the patience to stay in one place for very long, and his nature was too volatile. He was always off on his boat to the Caribbean or Europe, or traveling out West.

Sean left, saying good-bye to Lucy at the front door and leaving her with the two young children, my older brother and sister—I wasn't born yet. He stood there knocking his pipe on the brick, his hair freshly cut and his face buffed, looking immaculate, his Savile Row suit tailored to perfection, and his luggage the most expensive soft, brown suede. "Be a good girl," he said.

Shortly after Sean left, Rita informed Lucy that he wasn't going into town after all, but was out on his friend Larry Lander's yacht. Lucy's first instinct was: Oh good, a challenge. She would go after him, catch him! But something about Rita's news made the corners of Lucy's mouth turn down. She sat down on the couch and looked at her cousin in dismay. "So what will we do all weekend?"

Rita was curious about Lucy's reaction but she didn't want to be the one to fuss with the delicate balance of their marriage.

"There's plenty to do! How about going to the polo club or the country club and watching the tournament? Or we could go play some tennis."

Lucy interrupted her. She wanted to be where the real excitement was and had a plan. They would surprise Sean on the yacht! They spent the rest of that day plotting like two schoolgirls. Eventually they decided they would dress up as nuns. They found a costume store at a nearby town.

Rita's sharp face wasn't made for a habit. An animal cunning peered out from her brown eyes. Her appearance made Lucy laugh; she told Rita that she looked like a snake in a bonnet. Lucy, however, looked more like an angel that had been trapped in the dark cloth. Rita felt impaired by the material and kept poking at it with quick thrusts.

The evening was warm and filled with stars. When they arrived at the yacht club, they found it deserted. Rowboats lay on the dock like polished ribs. They slipped down the gangplank like two black spirits searching for Sean's soul with an old flashlight. They unhitched one of the rowboats and tumbled in. Rita insisted on rowing. They slid through the silent water out into the harbor and among the boats. Lucy perched herself on the gunwales of the bow like a dark gargoyle. The warm summer night swelled and the quiet boats at anchor held their masts and bowsprits like gentle swaying crosses high against the evening sky.

Lucy saw the boat at the far end of the harbor, a soft light glowing from it; she could just make out figures in the cockpit. They could hear loud masculine laughter, like drunken pirates enjoying their booty. Lucy smiled to herself, thinking of the reactions the men would have when they saw two nuns approaching in a rowboat.

As they gained quietly on the yacht, Lucy saw Sean standing in the open cockpit with another woman, whose red off-the-shoulder dress left little to the imagination, as did his drunken swaying. She had her arm draped around Sean and he was holding her close around the waist.

Rita tried to stop the boat but in her haste dropped the oar and sent the oarlock banging to the floor. Hearing the noise, Sean turned around, still holding the woman, and peered into the water below. The figures were so black that it was hard to make any details out. Then, as the rowboat moved closer, he must have made out two nuns, one sitting high on the bow.

The rowboat headed straight into the side of the bigger boat as the nun in the front instinctively put her hand out to avoid a collision. As Sean looked down on the scene before him, he perhaps thought for a moment that he saw his wife's face, the face of an angel that had just fallen from paradise. Then the strange little boat floated away and disappeared over the black water.

In that moment, betrayal flew out across the harbor and whistled mournfully through the boat's stays. From that moment, Lucy was never quite as beautiful as before. She was no longer the golden rich girl who captivated her young husband and tamed his restless male energy. She had been thrown away as lightly as if she'd never had any worth. Their grand wedding and their solemn vows were as ridiculous a mockery as her black habit. She was aware that her own actions had uncovered the very secret she couldn't face and would lead to a disastrous marriage for her.

That night on those dark waters was probably the beginning of the delicate balance of her mind slipping into thoughts of poison and sliding into chaos. As the boat slid back toward the dock, Lucy tore off her costume and threw it into the quiet water. It spread out over the reflected stars like a huge black bird.

4

Dreams and Conversations with God

Remember—know the experience of intimacy with God and God's protection when it was so desperately needed.
—Jerome Bernstein, Jungian analyst

I was born on my mother's bed, under the shadow of the cross of the Church of the Advent in Boston. It was the end of the Depression, which had no effect on our family life, as my father was in the oil and coal business in Boston. We had, for my first seven years, a community of help: Irish maids with flaming red hair and strong accents, a chauffeur, a cook, a laundress, and a nanny named Louise, whom I adored. I called her Eo. She came from "Novi," or Nova Scotia, and was a gentle, kind soul, who wouldn't play cards with me on Sundays. When I joined the adults for tea, I curtsied in my black velvet dresses with white lace collars, and had a combination of tea and milk, which I disliked. My life followed strict schedules, with meals in the nursery.

I was born the youngest child by ten years, and my father gave me the name Millicent after a waltz he particularly liked. By the time I was six, my sister and brother had gone to boarding school. We spent winters in Boston; summers at Crescent Island, my father's island, off the coast of Maine—the Middle Island; and long Easter vacations on Cumberland with my grandparents, Grandpa and Grandma Carnegie and family, until I was seven and World War II started.

The summer when I was six I was given my own bedroom on Crescent Island. It had a porch with window boxes of red geraniums and a powder-blue ceiling, and the echo of the sea bounced off the white walls of the house. I was over the kitchen, and in the early morning I could hear the rattle of the coal stove and smell the fresh bread being baked by Hannah, our Swedish cook. She made sand cookies the size of tablespoons out of cream, butter, and sugar. I tried to find her recipe again when I grew up, but couldn't, so they remain precious childhood memories.

It was on Crescent Island that I first heard the sound of the morning doves, calling me out of a night's sleep. I would lie in bed utterly content, hearing the doves' soft, melancholy sound, and wonder, as some children do, if it was really the sound of angels sifting through the first mourning light. I would watch with anticipation the white wooden wall of the house, as the sun crept across its edge and became luminous. I waited without moving, as the whiteness of the wall grew glowing in my mind, and listened to the constant hollow booming of waves echoing behind the wall. Then, one day, I saw the white nun form, her soft white habit waving and disappearing in the wall before she moved away mute and silent toward the sea.

I never forgot it. I felt I had seen something that was fiercely mysterious and slightly dangerous, for I couldn't see the face hidden in the hood. I put two pieces of wood together in the shape of a cross and hung them over my bed. I have no idea why; our family didn't go to church.

My father was very handsome in my eyes. He had a magnificent voice. He played the piano and banjo a bit and loved to sing. He would put a song on the old record player and I would get on my toes and dance and dance, or he would play something on the piano and I would join him. I particularly liked "My Melancholy Baby." My love of singing and yearning to be wrapped in music, even the music of nature and of the ocean, started early.

In those early summers my father would wake me up in the morning for our swim in the cold ocean with a song, "Good morning, Milly, don't you think it's silly to lie in bed on such a lovely day?" He taught me to swim by throwing me off the dock. To my amazement I rose to the surface and started a love affair with the sea. I spent the whole summer complaining bitterly that I wasn't a mermaid—could someone please do something about it so I could stay under the blue dome of the sea and watch the light dancing and playing through the water?

My father taught me, on stormy days, how to dive through the smooth, green, curled shell of the breaking waves and swim under the roaring, drowning bubbles above; perhaps he taught me something about surfing under chaos.

We would swim for miles out to sea. I would hang on his shoulder and when I got tired float a while. When we returned we would lie, like two beached whales, on the sand. He would say, "Open your mouth and let the sun get on your teeth," and I would open my mouth and bare my teeth to the sky because he said so.

He came back sometimes with treats and tricks from Daddy and Jacks, a store with jokes, puzzles, and tricks; I loved them. But one day he gave me a lump of sugar, which I immediately popped in my mouth. It had a dead fly in it. I was humiliated and disgusted and went behind a door and cried and cried. It was my first uneasy experience of my father. There were many more to come.

There was a sweet pony I was allowed to ride, and I was free to roam bareback on the beaches with cousins. One day in the early spring, my father took me riding by the Periwinkle River when all the wildflowers were in bloom and a new light greenness filled the woods and everything was quiet except for the birds singing. We stood on the cliff at the end of the river looking over the estuary, where the river made its way out to sea over long sweeps of sand and the lobstermen maneuvered carefully out of the crooked channel to pull their traps.

The hay barn held special attraction for us children, with its mountain of sweet, moldering, dusty hay. To slide from the top of that mountain into the pitch-black bottom and claw your way out to the sunlight was a daring adventure. We liked to go to the dairy to watch the fresh milk from the cows forming bubbles as it was poured into vats; or ride the horses over the breakwater's sand when the tide was dead low and explore the island that made a bay for Crescent Island and camp there overnight; or sail in little boats when the sea was calm; or pick bucketsful of blueberries on Blueberry Hill, overlooking the river as it floated down through the marshes; or swim in the path of the full moon, our bodies sparkling with phosphorescence as the sea splashed around us.

As the summers went by, the atmosphere in the house began to change; sometimes I would hear my mother and father fighting and would rush between them to try to stop them. One early morning, barely awake, I heard a loud sound coming through the porch of my room. At first I thought it must be the waves breaking like sharp strands of crystal on the rocks, except I had an odd feeling of dread. I reached the porch in time to see the broken remains of six milk bottles on the flagstone veranda and milk dripping from the wall where they'd been flung. The screen door flew open and a man appeared whom I could scarcely recognize as my father; the expression on his face was so distorted that he appeared to be in pain. In his large hands he carried three more milk bottles, which he raised above his head and smashed on the gray stone steps. He was shouting at no one in particular, orders that penetrated the entire house.

My father would not allow pasteurized milk in his house. He wanted the milk from the cows at his dairy—thick, rich, creamy, unpasteurized milk. His defense of this rather odd stance, he told me, was that while the men were pasteurizing the milk everyone sneezed into it. I believed him. It must have been frightening for Lucy to think the milk we were given was dangerous for all of us and not have any power to do anything about it.

That fear slowly turned into an obsession for Lucy. Sometime after the bottle-throwing incident I gave our beautiful, black, sweet-tempered Doberman pinscher, Sonia, a bowl of farm milk, as I often did. She died the next day. My mother told me that I had poisoned her. I felt terrible about Sonia and wondered why mother thought I had poisoned her, but I didn't talk to anyone about it. I was so ashamed. It was the beginning of my mother's obsession with poison. There were to be other obsessions too, including one about her Cumberland Island.

According to my mother (who told me when I was older), my father began bringing his mistresses to dine. This nasty habit continued through several other marriages, but then he added to it by bringing the mistresses' children, too. Later on, after my mother divorced him and he married a second time and had three children and acquired two stepchildren, he also acquired many lady friends, including the prospective third wife who, with her three children, kept drifting in and out of the house under the unsuspecting eyes of the second wife. He ended up with eleven children in total. My mother told me later that once, when a mistress showed up unannounced for dinner, she fainted onto her plate. I still have this childhood fantasy of my mother in a long, black, velvet off-the-shoulder dress falling in slow motion into her dinner.

When I tell people about my father's eleven children—for me, two whole siblings, three halves, and five steps—it sounds as if I'm reciting a recipe or a jazz number. In between wives were mistresses, and sometimes their children joined this rotating group, but this was all years later, after my mother divorced him.

Aunt Nan later told me the story of what happened in that last summer before World War II: "They had all gone to the country club to a dance on the mainland. Lucy couldn't have been more than in her late twenties. She loved to dance and enjoyed gentlemen. Sean, perhaps a bit drunk, looked over and saw her dancing with a particularly attractive man. He strode across the dance floor and pulled a fistful of Lucy's hair out, leaving a bald spot."

It was probably about this time that my dreams began, if they were dreams. Night after night with my eyes wide open, I would sink through the bed, then slowly, with my eyes still open, my long white nightgown swirling around me, I would find myself straddling a large wooden cross, still surrounded by the soft, thick blackness. I was quite comfortable and not at all afraid and knew that the cross was in the center of a large boat whose arching ribs surrounded me on either side. I could feel the boat rocking gently from side to side and hear it crack and moan. The boat's hold, like a smooth, bone-white, curling pelvis or chalice, held its cargo, sea chanting and rocking in its swelling ribs, and moved me through seawater that whispered against its sides, echoing sounds from distant lights and pole stars.

Holding firmly to the cross, I raised my head to the darkness and spoke with God. Night after night we talked, although I could never see Him, and when I came back through the bed and lay there, I could never remember what God had said, only the slight swish of falling stars rushing past and calling out, "Do not forget. Remember. Remember." But I couldn't remember, and would spend the rest of my life searching for hints and clues about what I had forgotten.

That summer I was sent away from the island to Beaver Camp, to keep me away from a marriage that was falling apart. At the age of six, I was the youngest child at the camp and, like all the other things in my short life that restricted my freedom, I found it disagreeable, as I was a tomboy, used to roaming around the island on my own. Also, I had to have a tutor while all the other children were acting or painting.

I hated being told what to do by adults—when to get up and when to go to bed and being marched out in the broiling sun in midis and bloomers to play softball. I loathed the atmosphere of togetherness. I enjoyed my friends, but I was a loner even then and always needed time alone.

Only the evenings of singing, swimming, and playing with friends were a joy. One rainy day, to escape the constant clatter of people—for we were always herded together as if a moment's solitude would endanger us—I crawled under a canoe that had been turned upside down among the pines. There, sitting with the rain softly rushing over my wooden roof with its gently curving beams, I felt there was a hint of my dream and maybe, I thought, I could remember. In the wonderful quiet I sat and sat, enveloped in the smell of pine needles, on a carpet of green moss.

Lunch passed and then dinner arrived. I was missing; no one could find me. Finally, as evening settled, I crawled out from under the canoe and wandered back to camp. There was lots of talk of me being expelled, of not getting a Beaver pin, of having to go before the Beaver board.

Confusion mixed with dread as I waited for the board to sentence me. When finally the time came, I stood before them, hanging my head, and kept repeating, "I don't know." I really didn't know why I had committed my crime, but I have felt that board sentence me many times since. It was the first time I ever felt what I would so often feel again throughout my life: that I was a stranger in the world. I couldn't have expressed it then, but later I came to believe that children who don't feel loved or cared for by their mothers at an early age wander through the world without the connections to it that others have—not understanding that they're estranged.

I got sick after my sentencing and was taken to the infirmary, where I slept for two straight days, exhausted from the effort of trying to live in this world. The war came after that summer and we left our house by the edge of the sea, and Mother and I returned alone to Boston as my father joined the navy. I missed my island terribly.

5

Dust

People told me my mother was beautiful. By the time I was able to perceive her face, I only saw the mouth turned sharply down at the edges and a glimpse of wildness in her eyes.

When mother and I returned to the Boston house after the summer, the help were still there to keep it dusted and clean and to serve meals. Then, little by little, things began to change. It was 1941, and the two cheerful Irish maids, Tina and Annie, left for better war jobs. Hannah, the cook, was getting old and found it too hard to manage without them, so she soon left. Others followed. There was no gas for the chauffeur, and the house began to fill with a ringing silence that was disturbing.

My father and brother went off to the war in 1941. My sister found another family and lived with them. I didn't see my father for the next six years. My mother divorced him and left him to his ladies. The war years were the best of his life, he later said. He was stationed on an island in the South Sea, responsible for a nurses' unit.

Eo, my nanny, had left when I was five and started nursery school. She came back after everyone else left, to my delight. One day about a month after she returned, we were walking in the Boston Common when Eo turned to me and said, "Millicent, I have to tell you something." I grabbed the soft upper part of her arm from which she usually shook me off. "I'm leaving," she said.

"But why, Eo, why?"

"It's your mother, I can't be around her." Even at that age

I was amazed, for Eo never said a bad thing about anyone. I was devastated and wept for days.

By the time I was seven, all the help had left, some to better war jobs, some out of fear of my mother's outbursts and often odd behavior. I lived alone with her in that large house in Boston for the next seven years. I don't know which I became aware of first, the slow disintegration of my mother's mind or the dust settling on the empty house with its sweet acid smell.

She had two persistent themes to which I didn't answer back—I already knew that it was dangerous and I wouldn't win. She said that I was a rape baby. (I didn't understand what a "rape baby" was, except that it was some way my father had hurt her.) I didn't understand that maybe she didn't want me. She also said that I was full of poison, poisoned by the unpasteurized milk from my father's farm. I soon learned to avoid conversations with my mother at all costs. I knew it would end with her two themes and she would win. I also became accustomed, very quickly, to understanding that there would be no more meals, just odd things like shad roe and cocktail cheeses in a cold icebox. On the dark evenings, she took to sitting motionless in the large chair by one of the windows or standing behind the maroon velvet curtains in the living room entrance.

Little by little, hardly realizing it, I was moving into that other world of silence, dreams, and daydreams. Slowly over the years, in my childhood dreams and psyche, I felt I made connections to the other side, and I learned things others didn't seem to know. I started watching myself and others from a distance. Sometimes I yearned for freedom from their world and their strange ways, and I began to make decisions inside myself. It became a habit not to listen to what people said because it had nothing to do with what I wanted and needed, and besides, I preferred my world a thousand times to theirs. Still, I watched with fascination to see how they behaved so I could pretend and act like that too. I could never really get the hang of it and was puzzled by how they learned to behave so naturally, so comfortably protective of their right to be here. Then I would give up and fall back on my daydreams and stiffly turn my head away from adults.

The silence shifting through the dust in the house began to feel dangerous. I began locking myself in my room. I couldn't leave like the others had. I never liked the house, but my favorite room was the green room. It had high ceilings and light lettuce-colored walls with long, silk chartreuse curtains that fell in puddles on the floor. There was a grand piano, which I spent hours coaxing sounds out of, and elegant French and Italian antiques. Most important of all, I was fascinated by the beautiful mirror over the fireplace with its gold frame, smoky glass, and black spots where the mirror had worn out. I loved to look in it and imagine other worlds.

But gradually I became afraid of looking in the mirror, and started turning my face away from adults and teachers. I didn't want them to see my eyes. I became terrified as the years went on that if I looked in the mirror, I wouldn't see my reflection, but my mother's face staring back at me, smiling slightly, and perhaps, without knowing it, I would sense she wanted me to die. Even more frightening, though, was my fear that I would look in the mirror and see no one at all.

6

Driftings

Sorrow is the servant of the intuitive.
—Rumi

About two years after the servants left, the driftings began. The house slowly became covered with black city grit, wrapped in cobwebs, and adorned with rotting silk curtains, filthy windows, and empty iceboxes. I started to dream that I opened the icebox door and was bitten by a vicious, slimy creature. The house was silent and totally isolated from the outside world—and filled with traps! If demons and fiends exist, they lay waiting in dark corners. Danger, always danger. Heavy maroon velvet curtains hid Lucy, who would stand behind them and listen, then float through the house or up to the attic without a sound, or sit in a dark room without moving.

Lucy had hired a lovely lady, Mrs. Whighton, a Christian Scientist and secretary, who came in once a month or so. She made sure I got my monthly allowance. She filled rows of black notebooks, full chapters, about poison milk, undulant fever (or brucellosis, its medical name for the illness caused by unpasteurized milk), and how I behaved because of it. My mother invented this idea that I had undulant fever so that she could accuse my father in court of poisoning his child, as she was in the process of divorcing him. Mrs. Whighton left when I went to boarding school. I remember mother was awfully cruel to her. Perhaps she had stayed on to help me. She came to mother's funeral and told me something I was to hear so many times: "I couldn't stay any longer—your mother was frightening."

Lucy started coming home at odd hours of the night, then

often not at all. In later years I learned she was "working" at the Officers' Club in the Common, greeting the boys and the wounded as they got off the boats. I do remember her learning to put bandages on me, which was fun. Lucy said she had always wanted to be a doctor. She had times that made it seem *as if* everything was all right; but it wasn't. That "as if" behavior lasted almost to the end of her life, when anyone could see clearly that she wasn't well, but until then it was impossible to explain to people who met her socially and didn't know her well, or to my teachers, that my mother was often quite mad.

I remember years later, when I was eighteen, my Aunt Nan took me to a psychiatrist, as my professors at college felt I needed help. He explained the "as if" personality—the psychiatric term for people whose identities are fluid: they can appear fine one minute and frightening the next. For instance, Lucy would be working with Mrs. Whighton and she would suddenly start screaming at her.

When I got older, it was hard to avoid noticing that she was greatly interested in men. Even when I was a child of about twelve or thirteen (during the war), she often didn't come home from the Officers' Club at night. I think she was incapable of feeling love, but she also left me with the feeling that men were an important part of one's happiness. When she got very upset she would have nosebleeds, trailing drops of blood on the stairs or on a desk, and leaving blood-soaked handkerchiefs in small red balls around the house.

Lucy didn't appear to mind that everyone had left.

It was the nights that were devastating. I tried to get home before dark. I had a little gold cross on a gold chain, and the key to the house hung around my neck on a dirty piece of string. I was afraid of losing it and being locked out. I'd let myself in and make a dash for my room. At all costs, if Mother was home, I wanted to avoid her in the dark. Safely in my room, I would slam shut the black bars of the

Spanish locks, my skin and muscles tightening as I gasped for breath, hair raised on the back of my neck in fear. I felt like an animal.

I stayed in my room listening to the music from my little white radio. Its melodies and minor tunes kept coaxing me back to earth—coaxing me to feel things as I looked out my window at the cross on the steeple of the Church of the Advent, solid against the sky. I seldom got to sleep until around 4:00 A.M. I lay in bed and waited and watched and thought and thought. I was trying to figure it all out so I could survive. I started banging my head against the wall, asleep or awake, until it hurt. As it got dark, I'd think I heard a noise outside the door, and I'd sit there on the bed wondering if that evil energy could slide under the locked door. Did Lucy wander through the house carrying a knife? I wasn't altogether sure where Lucy would draw the line. Like those primitive sorcerer-priests who killed their enemies by waving a bone at them, she was dangerous and powerful. But I kept an unspoken truce between us in spite of the fact that my simplest needs—food, clothing, attention, love—were not met.

Over time, I was removed too long from the usual influences of society and relatives to understand that the affluent often felt more self-important than the poor; I only saw that there were kind people and unkind ones, crazy people and supposedly sane ones.

I was unseen by my mother and by the people around me—as though I didn't really exist. I learned to arrange my face into what I assumed was a normal expression. But I couldn't stop my eyes from being full of pain. I was also relieved that against my wishes some part of me betrayed how sad I was.

I was moving more and more into the world of fantasy, symbolism, and metaphor. Eventually, when the pressure became too overwhelming, I felt as if I had moved out of my body altogether to a place where no one could reach or touch me. I could watch everything from the outside, ice cold, and safe, but still hearing the north wind whisper of fear. I became a girl who had lost all other feeling, a girl who was no longer able to express her anger.

I think it was about then that I observed my friends with wonder, trying to understand how they had come to feel so comfortable in the world. I had moments when I simply lost the ability to understand how to behave: where to put my eyes, my arms, and my body. I believe this is when I started disconnecting from people and sensing that I didn't belong in the world.

School became a problem; I started flunking my classes. I tried to hide in the back row, dripping with perspiration, so afraid I'd be asked a question that I would go numb and speechless, and longed to be back in my room where no one could see me. I was captain of the soccer team and made lots of friends among the "unpopular" girls. I knew how they felt.

In music class I loved to sing and was sometimes asked to sing a little something on my own. I started singing in my friend's Unitarian Church choir. She was the minister's daughter and lived next door. Lucy tried to stop me from singing in the choir but I wouldn't let her. My singing had nothing to do with her. It was a gift from another place and I wasn't going to let her take it away from me. She called the minister and said she didn't want me to sing in the choir anymore. It was one of the few confrontations I ever had with her. Standing on the stairs, I shouted that she couldn't stop me, then ran to my room and slammed the lock on my door shut. I continued to sing in the choir, but I started to sound a little flat, as if fingers were squeezing my neck.

I loved to write too, especially as there was no one for me to talk to in the house. I wrote and wrote all my feelings, secrets, and conversations with myself. I hid the notebooks under the bed until, one day, they all disappeared. I was crushed, but I didn't want to ask Lucy if she had taken them. It didn't stop me from writing, though, and I loved to read—my favorite story was the children's version of *At the Back of the North Wind* by George MacDonald. It is about a little boy called Diamond who lives in a loft above a horse barn. The North Wind begins to visit him at night. "Her hair fell down all about her till her face looked out of the midst of it like a moon out of a cloud." She is the most beautiful lady he has ever seen. Sometimes they dance and sometimes she takes him in her arms and they travel over rivers, land, mountains, and the sea, and when Diamond looks up at her he sees the loving eyes of a great lady. "The next moment her black hair went streaming out from her as she flung herself abroad in space amongst the stars with Diamond." One day the North Wind sinks a boat and all the sailors perish. Diamond is very upset and afraid, but she holds him next to her heart and explains that is what she is and does and she bears it: "Through all the noise I hear the sound of a far off song and music and it is quite enough to make me able to bear the cry from the drowning ship." In the end Diamond asks the North Wind, who terrifies him, yet whom he loves very much, to take him home, but not to his old home. That's how he goes to live at the back of the North Wind where she sits on a throne of blue ice and crystal icicles filled with sparks of lights, in the land of death. The North Wind—death—became my teacher.

Since there was little food in the house, I ate at school, had dinner at the drugstore, and stole candy bars from subway newsstands. As the years went by, my clothes got smaller and smaller and worn out. My polo coat had large threadbare patches around the buttonholes where the white inner lining showed through. A friend of Aunt Nan's saw me one day on the street and called her, using words like *vagabond* and *orphan* to describe me. I soon received a care package from my father, delicious clothes fit for one's mistress, slinky black dresses and a leopard-print scarf.

I often sat on endless train rides to sitters' homes or to my Aunt Nan's in Greenwich, Connecticut, where I spent several summers and holidays and weekends. On dark, rainy nights in the reflection of the train window, I couldn't distinguish the raindrops from my tears—nor could I have expressed the devastating thought that I simply wasn't wanted.

For two summers at the beginning of the war, I was sent to live with my grandfather, Andrew Carnegie II, on the North Shore outside of Boston. Grandmother had died and Grandpa and I were in a big house by ourselves with a nurse for him and the servants. There was no one to play with except my grandfather, a very dear man whom I liked very much.

We enjoyed each other's company, but there were times when I upset him. I was always climbing on the roof; once I was caught by Grandfather, who heard a noise and came out with a gun. Other times I slept at night under the magnolia bushes, to be found on his morning walk, or sneaked out of the house at 4:00 A.M. to climb an enormous pine tree and watch the first light. In the early fall, when it came time to go back to school in Boston, I would walk a mile to the nearby railroad station. It was hardly a station really; there was no station house, just an unused parking lot. I would stand near the track and hail down the engineer to stop. Sometimes there were one or two others, but usually that big train stopped just for me.

My sister came to see Mother and me once, soon after I arrived back in Boston for school. She got into a terrible battle with Mother—something I had learned instinctively never to do, as I knew one couldn't win with her and it could be frightening to deal with a mind over the edge, out of control. On this occasion Mother, who was wearing a long, green velvet dressing gown, got down on the floor on all fours and started crawling toward my sister, swinging her head from side to side as she screamed, "You have always tried to murder me, always tried to kill me, always, always!" To be accused of murdering my mother would have been more than I could bear. My sister backed away and left immediately and didn't come back.

Soon after that incident my Aunt Nan sent up a Trappist nun who had left her abbey after having lived there in silence for years. She was a small, stiff, stern sort who wore shoulder pads. I still have the letter she sent to my aunt: "I have never been through or witnessed anything like it in my life. I cannot stay here one more moment." These words had become a kind of litany that would continue for the rest of Mother's life, a sentiment repeated again and again by others who came to stay.

As I never spoke with anyone about my life with Lucy, I became inarticulate about what I felt. I think it was around this period of my life that I lost a sense of time, the sequence of things that most people have. It never occurred to me to mention that I was miserable and didn't know what to do about flunking so many courses or being so afraid when I sang my solo on Sunday that I would be hoarse and the tiniest bit off-key. I just rearranged my face again for the world until I could take it all back to my room and my cross and my river and the people walking by under the window. In my imagination the cross flew across the sky and said, "It is proper to suffer." The cross in some supernatural way not only gave its protection and special meaning to my circumstances, but also held up its iron arms against my anger.

Great Vows

When I was about nine, Mother hired an accommodator, a person who comes for a month, or one day a week. I called her Cookie. She was Irish and had silver hair touched with yellow and plump fingers. She moved into the basement. I wasn't allowed to go in the kitchen, which was in the basement, so I seldom saw her, and in any case I hated the kitchen. There were narrow stairs painted deep blue going down to it. It was below ground level and dark, and the furnace sounded like a human heart, beating away. There was a heavy breathing sound. Cookie was to become one of the long list of people who came and left in a hurry.

One day when I got home, I ran upstairs as usual and locked the doors to my room and bathroom. Cookie was to put my dinner in the elevator on a tray at 6:00 P.M., and I was to ring it up. One night just before 6:00, I heard a knock on the door, and Cookie asking to come in. She was carrying my tray and weaving around a bit. She told me to sit on the bed and proceeded to feed me burned spinach, spoonful by spoonful. I ate it partly out of bewilderment and partly because I sensed that for her it was an act of kindness; there was a shared but unspoken sense of danger between us in this house. The next night I rang for the tray and nothing happened. Finally, I summoned up my courage and went down the four flights of stairs. "Cookie," I called out. No answer, just a heavy silence. When I arrived at the kitchen door, I found her. She was lying under the kitchen table. Her body lay in a pool of blood, one arm flung out from her side with a large carving knife next to it; she wasn't moving.

As usual I couldn't find Mother anywhere, so I fled upstairs and called my friend next door, the minister's daughter. The ambulance came, and they took Cookie. She was never mentioned by anybody again. I don't know if it was a suicide, but it looked like it to me. I have no idea if they even found my mother before they took Cookie away. I had gone to my room.

I couldn't sleep that night, so I pushed my bed over to the window in order to watch the world below. I tuned my old-fashioned little white radio to play its endless round of popular songs, and placed my stuffed animal, Dazzle, carefully on the windowsill. Dazzle had been with me for at least six years. He was made of gray and white crocheted wool and might have been a mouse except his nose was too long and made him look more like an anteater with long ears.

It became a ritual. Having set my kingdom in order, I would arrange my long white nightgown and place my elbows on the windowsill and observe the world. It was by far the best time of day because it was too late to do anything else, even my homework (which I never did), and I liked being alone.

My window above the world looked out over brick houses and slate rooftops, old city streets that emptied onto the esplanade where soldiers and their girls, old men, dogs, and people of all varieties enjoyed walking in the grass and sitting on park benches.

Beyond the park was the river that ran through the city and under the Salt-and-Pepper Bridge. This is what it was called because it had four stone towers at either end that looked like old-fashioned silver salt- and pepper shakers. Above all this was the Carter's Inn Clock, which lit up at night in wonderful green and orange colors, except for the time itself, which shone forth in a luminous white. I thought it was a marvelous thing that someone had donated that clock so that all the people in the city could see the time.

And I would watch my river roll by the esplanade, and the cross on the Church of the Advent race against the clouds and the sky.

I sat there talking to Dazzle, who had a magnificent gift of silence, my elbows digging into the hard, dirty rim of the window until they were well worked with sore red lines. As the evening moved by below, the mood and feeling of the city changed, the people went home, the air seemed lighter, and the rather sickly smell of a warm city disappeared, but most of all the quality of light changed as if the darkness might succeed in blotting everything out before the dawn. As I sat there, I found myself thinking over the day's events.

For quite some time now I had the feeling small animals must have when constantly attacked by large predatory beasts, a kind of constant alert, a raising of the fur and a sniffing for the odor of danger or fear. Suddenly the world was becoming unpredictable, and it was getting harder to compete with the growing importance of the poison in my mother's mind. I was being squeezed out of the grown-up world, and my place of "becoming" was my seat by the window. Sitting there contemplating these things, I found myself feeling it was important to decide what kind of person I should be: *How should I react? How do I want to fit in? Should I be good or bad?* I was convinced I had a choice.

I pictured myself swaggering down the school hall, my Scottish kilt swinging wildly behind me, dragging my dirty, green book bag, broadcasting in my walk that I was mean and tough. Then when I got home, I would say things to hurt Lucy, scream back at the endless confusion—viciously. But I kept thinking I didn't want to be vicious.

Something drew my attention back to the city scene in front of me—some subtle occurrence, an unusual ringing sound, a shift of light, I'm not quite sure what. It was very late, perhaps around 4:00 or 5:00 P.M. Everything was quiet; all the cars and people had disappeared. The river looked

black and more mysterious as it rolled under the bridge and
the Carter's Inn Clock stood out by itself; all the other lights
had been turned off. Silence seemed to blanket the city in
an eerie stillness. Captured and folded into its soft, black
feathers, I didn't move, didn't even breathe, but sank slowly
to a silent place, where if I knew how to look and listened
hard enough, I felt I could hear a whisper or a secret or
perhaps even an answer. It was my first glimpse that maybe
there were other worlds, something inside, an inner voice
or something perhaps sacred in the silence. It was the first
time, since my dream as a young child of talking to God,
that I felt that subtle longing—not for a mother, but for
something I couldn't define.

Perhaps it was a place where great rivers flowed quietly through space and clocks filled with light told time
without ticking and floated over sleeping cities, and where
the morning light shifted and tangled and pushed at the
blackness—pushed to come back and give new shapes and
forms to things again.

"The Star-Spangled Banner" suddenly blared out from
the radio. Startled and by now very tired, I picked up Dazzle,
hugging him so tightly that his loose stuffing bulged in
yet another spot, crawled under the covers, and whispered
into Dazzle's ear, "It's all right, Dazzle, I'm not crazy. I
am going to be good."

8

Poisonous

Lucy decided to put me in the hospital when I was about eleven, two years after Cookie disappeared, to have me "cleaned out" of the poisonous, milky substance. Then she could write long letters to her lawyers, to judges, her relatives, friends, Aunt Nan and doctors telling how her ex-husband had poisoned me so that I was seriously ill and in the hospital.

I found myself standing at the entrance to the scrubbed and clean-smelling ward, my two brown braids neatly pulled behind me, thinking, "I feel fine. What if they find out I am fine?" I was afraid I would be caught in the lie, and even if it wasn't my lie, I felt humiliated. Glancing down the rows of beds, I saw only older women. Occasionally, some beds were separated by a glass partition, but for the most part there was just a white curtain.

A nurse led me to a large private room that looked out directly onto the wall of another building. Lucy followed us in, inspected the room, and put down my bag and schoolbooks.

"You'll feel better soon," Lucy informed me. "You know your test was positive. You have undulant fever from the milk, but Dr. Tobin says he can help you."

I turned my head away from my mother. "I don't want to stay here," I whispered.

"You're a very sick girl." With that, Lucy left. I didn't see her again for the three weeks that I stayed in the hospital. There were no visitors, and it never occurred to me to call anyone. Whom would I call? I was forbidden to see any of my fathers' relatives by Mother. She had made that very clear to them too, and during the war, men left, and often wives, if possible, followed them to army camps.

The hospital was a teaching hospital, so I saw a great many interns. They came to study me, a specimen of undulant fever, a sickness brought on by unpasteurized milk. They kept asking me questions, and I kept saying that I felt fine. I seemed to have a lot of colds, but that was all. Sitting all day by myself in a room with nothing to do but read or look at the walls, I felt as if I were being punished. The doctors, serious and in a hurry, wearing their white coats and carrying the authority of God, told me I was being tested for undulant fever, and that they were going to try out a new drug on me. I took it all in and began to feel overwhelmed by the authority of these doctors who agreed with my mother. What if it were true? I began to grind my teeth, often without realizing it, and I sang a little singsong litany against the doctors whom I did not like or trust and against Lucy, whom I didn't trust either: "The milk is not poison, the milk is not poison."

Lucy had talked about this disease as if it were dangerous, as if it could kill people and dogs, and I wondered, in spite of myself, what it was that made the doctors believe my mother. Lucy had told me that her friend Carlyle's feet had turned black and that she had died from it, and now these men took it seriously. What bothered me the most was that they believed my mother. To people she met casually, Lucy was believable.

After five days of tests and sitting in my private room alone, I asked to be allowed to go to the ward. The doctors in their wisdom, or curiosity, had decided to give me injections of the newly discovered drug penicillin, every two hours, night and day. By the second day my arms were sore, but moving into the ward at least provided some distractions and lots of attention. In spite of myself I wanted to please these doctors who seemed interested in me; I enjoyed and delighted in the unusual attention, but I was puzzled. My father had insisted I drink the milk when we lived on the island. Why would these important doctors keep me in the hospital if nothing were wrong? I couldn't sort it out, I became confused and the confusion kept going around and around in my head.

The nurses gave me odd jobs to do, and a large Italian lady named Sophie took me under her wing. Sophie had few inhibitions and would laugh and holler and waddle up and down the ward, a large cross swaying from her neck, talking with all the patients in broken English. She had had a serious operation, and I guessed from the conversations of the nurses, which I sometimes overheard, that she was not at all well. Next to my bed was an old lady with gray hair who hardly ever spoke. She died in the night, and there were lots of whispers as they took her away.

After two weeks my body became sore all over from the injections. The nurses tried to find new places to inject the new drug. The nighttime was the time I disliked the most. After being woken up for the injection, I would lie in bed, watching the nurse walk around the ward in her soft, gummy shoes. There was just enough light to see the outlines of the beds and the warm glow of the nurses' station at the end of the corridor. I would lie there and think to myself, *I am not ill. I do not have undulant fever. I am perfectly healthy. I am not full of poison, I am not full of poison, I am not full of poison*. But what I couldn't say to myself and what began to form in my mind was, *What if I am full of poison? What if I am bad?*

9

Pre–Boarding School

Suffering brings intuition.
—Rumi

The same year I was put in the hospital, I was dropped back a year at school. I had several good friends in the class, but I left the class of my two best friends, both ministers' daughters: Hope, the Unitarian minister's daughter who lived nearby, with whom I sang in the choir, and Addy at the Church of the Advent, where my cross flew against the sky.

There was no gas because of the war, so we went to school together on the subway instead of being driven by the chauffeur. We often spent hours discussing God, crawling all over the outdoor concert shell on the esplanade and pretending we were famous actors from its stage, or playing hide-and-seek in the church pews. Sometimes I went with Addy to have dinner with the nuns who were connected to the Church of the Advent, which was very high Episcopalian. About a year later, Lucy called their mothers and said I shouldn't play with them anymore. I don't know what she said but I lost my two friends. Their mothers didn't want me to play with them anymore.

I felt strange dropping back a class and meeting a whole new group of classmates, and I felt ashamed that they would all know I was so dumb. But in the spring, I started getting up very early when the weather was good and roller-skated to school down the esplanade and then through the streets. It was about ten miles to school and wonderful in the early light to have that freedom to slide by my river. Sometimes on the weekends I would ride the subways for miles, often with my friends, until we were in the suburbs, and I invented a game to see how many blocks we could go without being seen by anyone. I was also a good athlete and was made captain of the basketball team and the forthcoming President of my class, to my surprise. I thought perhaps they felt sorry for me because I was older.

I came to treasure being alone, where I could let my emotions go and weep if I wanted to and not be fearful as I was all day, trying to cope with people and teachers and school and what I was feeling. At times I felt there was also a very calm quietness in me, which probably helped me survive, a connection maybe through my intuition and a developing psychic ability. Perhaps all that pain was the beginning of thinking in metaphors, creating a symbolic world rather than a real one—something that made me look at this world differently than others. I couldn't understand then that without having been cared for and loved and mothered, one could not know what it's like to be loved, to live in such a world. Sometimes I found tremendous joy in life and its beauty and the need to express myself, none of which had anything to do with who my parents were, my circumstances, or school. I could get up and roller-skate down by my river in complete freedom.

Other times, alone in those nights, I tried so hard to understand that my mind went over and over what was happening to me with no answers but my own. In my room I locked myself into my frantic mind, into fear and a terrible intensity, with an unhealthy stiffening of muscles. I was alert to constant danger, and I kept banging my head on the wall.

It was about this time that my mother announced I would be going to Grove Hall, a boarding school in the Virginia horse country. I was relieved to be leaving, though I didn't have the least idea of what Grove Hall would hold for me.

10

Boarding School

To know no fear
(of the final end)
To reach for light
I ask
No more
—Millicent (age 14)

Grove Hall was a boarding school of family tradition, and there was a long line of women on both sides of my family, cousins, aunts, my sister, and children of great friends of the family who had been going there for years. It wasn't my decision that I should go there; there was no thought about if it was right for me. That was never discussed between me and my mother or father or anyone. At the time it seemed to me it might be an escape. In some ways it was—I was released from my room.

When I arrived there, I found it to be a place lacking in charm and beauty. Grove Hall came into existence in part because of the country's great robber barons, in the 1920s, when girls were expected not to work but to marry well— rather like Wallis Simpson, who proved without beauty or wealth that she could succeed. She was perhaps amongst the most clever of the female robber barons.

It was an all-female school of about eighty girls, with Miss Mansfield as its headmistress, in the fox-hunting country of Virginia. I did not care for horses. One year I had two roommates who rode: one was Sister Parish's daughter, who would decorate Jackie Kennedy's White House, and the other was a Mellon, who eventually graduated from Radcliffe and died young. Both were avid hunters; they would bring me back a little manure and straw for a good laugh. Among the very well off, the top percentile, there was no place for a budding artist or the student who might have to support herself upon leaving. In the 1950s at Grove Hall, there was little appreciation of the arts, ballet, opera, or poetry. In fact, someone with a strong artistic talent might have been considered slightly suspect. We were hermetically sealed and packaged for a good marriage and children, and any psychiatric problems that existed among us were either not understood or simply ignored.

The rich and the powerful sent their children to be among other rich children with a very clear message: this is the correct society to be in—do not venture outside. We expect you to marry one of your own, and when the time is right we will provide coming-out parties so that you can meet appropriate husbands. Some of us were a bit like the kittens who in the first six months of a study were kept in a room that had vertical stripes, and upon being released into a horizontal world found they couldn't walk.

In my first year, I was put in the dorm of the class ahead of me and had two respected roommates. Miss Mansfield, the headmistress, told me it was because I was a leader, and it would be good for me. One roommate, after a life that included frightening poverty, would end up running the Fulbright Foundation. She eventually married Senator Fulbright in his old age. After he died, Clinton appointed her executive director of the President's Committee on the Arts and the Humanities.

Another roommate became Princess of Luxembourg, and, after her prince died, the Duchess de Mouchy. During our senior year, we got into a bad hair-pulling, scratching fistfight in the dorm because she said she was going to get our English teacher, my mentor, Mr. Carr, dismissed. I said, over my dead body. The housemother and other girls had to separate us to stop us from pulling each other's hair out. I always did admire her as a powerful personality.

Then there was a quiet, dark-haired, very intelligent girl who went to Radcliffe. She and her husband flew over the Atlantic in a small plane and never came back, leaving three children. I had no idea she was wealthy, probably one of the wealthiest in the country, or that our ancestors had been in business together. In fact, I never thought at all about being a Carnegie. If anything, I was one of the Boston girls who didn't have the same clout as the New York girls.

There are many kinds of privilege. There is the privilege of wealth, earned and unearned. This allows you time to do as you wish, wisely or unwisely. You may enjoy freedom if you know how to use it; education if you desire to pursue it; beauty if you know how to appreciate it; philanthropy if you believe in it; and exploration if you crave it. There is the privilege of health, or of being handsome or beautiful. There is the privilege of being very talented or brilliant in your field. There is also the privilege of being an artist.

Faced with privilege or pain, we didn't know why they were bestowed on us. We were not allowed to choose. Some of my peers were given gifts they could not use; some had enormous good fortune, some endless pain, but being brought up in the cocoon of wealth leaves one sealed off from many realities: the importance of money, class snobbery, the need to earn a living, the instability of one's place in the world. Did we consider ourselves special? Were we naïve, thoughtless, hollow? Some, maybe. For most, there was an unconscious certainty that life would be an easy ride, but I don't think many of us were even aware of the enormous privilege we were born into; we just expected things to continue as they always had.

When I arrived at Grove Hall, I was stunted in my emotional development. Much of the time I simply couldn't function. Again, I would sit in class hoping not to be noticed. I couldn't understand why I had to learn the endless dates of when men rushed out to kill each other. I was interested in why they did it. I had little interest in what the school had to teach, and in my sophomore year I flunked every midterm exam.

I became a problem. The faculty at Grove Hall seemed to think I behaved the way I did on purpose. I was put in a study by myself and taken out of the glee club and octet, which I loved—a terrible blow that didn't help my marks. I was too independent and a bit of a troublemaker; I'd pull stunts like trying to make distilled cider in the attic in a barrel that exploded one evening.

One time a girl and I were walking toward our dorm when we turned around to see a rabid fox (there had been warnings) following us. The fox bit the girl and flew through the dorm door. I hollered for everyone to close their doors and followed the fox into the living room, where I found my best friend, Tilly, standing on the piano, trapped by the fox that was pacing below. I ran to the infirmary to tell the staff, but no one would believe me. It took some convincing.

Not once in my four years did anyone on the faculty ask me if anything was the matter—not that I could have expressed it then, even if they had.

Then several good things happened. My mother got married; Mr. Carr, my English and singing teacher, took me under his wing; and, to my amazement, I became president of my class. I was in the infirmary with a wretched case of poison ivy when a group of my classmates came and brought me the news. At the time, all I could think was, *Well, the faculty will certainly be amazed or upset.* Maybe my election was because Miss Mansfield had announced I had leadership qualities; or because of my odd and different point of view as one outside the confines of the school environment; or because of the empathy I felt for those who, like myself, had been miserable. Whatever the reasons, I was amazed, puzzled, and pleased, and immediately started thinking about how to do a good job. I began to get good marks and I had a few friends, including one whose father was a Theosophist (he ran Wendell Willkie's campaign and wrote a book called *Bridge Between Two Worlds*). From her came the flowering of my fascination with the world of the spirit, the spiritual—not the religious—life. We would shut ourselves in the linen closet after everyone had gone to bed and spend hours discussing the life of the spirit. I was fascinated by Rudolf Steiner, the founder of theosophy; I read his book, *Knowledge*, along with the works of Annie Besant, who believed you could see a Christ-like halo around people who were spiritually evolved.

When Lucy remarried, I was relieved of the burden of caretaker. But I felt sorry for her, too; I worried that if I deserted her, she might die. None of the family, except eighty-year-old Aunt Bebe and I, attended the wedding. I was delighted to escape from school, as we were only given one weekend off in four years, aside from Christmas and Easter. The wedding took place in Aunt Bebe's very elegant house with just four of us and a friend of Mother's. She told me a bit about Jack, Mother's new husband. It was obvious he wasn't all there, but he was a dear human being. I was told he was a manic-depressive, a term used in those days, and, like my great-grandmother, had been in McLean. It meant nothing to me. I learned that he was taken care of by friends and relatives who provided him an office in Boston where he had nothing to do. One morning when he was waiting for the train to go to his office, his briefcase unsnapped: in front of everyone was an empty briefcase holding only a roll of toilet paper, which rolled out, bounced to the edge of the platform, and fell across the tracks like a great white scar.

I was now old enough to be somewhat independent. Before I was seven, our family had been one of the first in the country to ski—there were no lifts, so we put skins on our skis and climbed up the slopes. I spent vacations skiing with friends and their families. Once at Sun Valley with friends, I met a nice young Canadian who was a member of the Fédération Internationale de Ski (F.I.S.) team. I was soon skiing with the team; it was a marvelous vacation. I spent part of the summer at Crescent Island with my father's new family, his two stepchildren and three young children; I loved the times I spent there, except for the growing understanding that all was not well with him. I learned he had enormous energy and charm, but also a very angry, violent side.

Mother had left the house in Boston and moved with Jack to my Grandfather Carnegie's summerhouse on the North Shore, and things went better for her for a number of years after her marriage to Jack. When I was with Lucy, she chartered a racing boat for me, and I would bicycle the six or seven miles to the yacht club, which became my home away from home.

Later she and Jack gave me a coming-out party, as did my father. Lucy took me to New York, where we stayed at the Sherry-Netherland for a couple of days and bought some dresses for the season. It was fun, and Mother's great social manners and wit were at their best. Those who aren't familiar with mental illness don't realize there are sometimes periods when those affected can be or seem normal, which makes the illness in some ways more devastating because there is hope. Like a fatally ill cancer patient in remission, my mother benefited—if only temporarily—from the "as if" syndrome. Years later I came across this observation from Lillian Hellman: "A crazy person is crazy all of the time. I have frequently found this valuable when in the company of a crazy person who is, for the moment, lucid."

Back at Grove Hall, I couldn't fathom all the tradition, the strange "school worship"—like making a circle and singing praises to Grove Hall. Tradition had absolutely no place in my world, but I didn't mind wearing khaki Women's Army

Corps (WAC) uniforms and drilling with guns four times a week; or being at what appeared to be a military school with lots of mud and horses and generals reviewing us; or sleeping out on open porches with ponchos over our beds.

In my senior year, under Mr. Carr's tutelage, I sang a solo in front of the whole school and, to my surprise, got a standing ovation. This moved Miss Mansfield to rise up, shake my hand, and say, "Now finally you have done something for Grove Hall." And I thought, *No, I have done something for myself.*

I left feeling my four years were wasted, but I was accepted at Sarah Lawrence College and didn't return to my mother's for very long that summer. I had not dealt with what was haunting me. At Grove Hall the old feelings of disliking being told what to do and being constantly around groups of people came back. Nothing in the educational system excited me except for Mr. Carr's English class and singing lessons, which I loved. Unfortunately, I was not a Grove Hall girl.

11

Coming-Out Parties, College, and Musical Ambitions

The summer was taken up by coming-out parties and being with friends. My mother was not really part of my life at this point, especially as I had been sent away so often, so it felt natural to stay with friends or with my father and his new family. At that time I didn't know anything about mental illness or that Mother would get worse or that my primary role, when I had one, would be to care for her. But that summer after boarding school, I was free. I fell in love twice. The first time was with a boy who had eyes like the devil, slightly slanted and fiercely browed. I had seen him across the table at a coming-out party in Boston and started scheming about how to get to know those eyes better. It turned out that he was kind and gentle and brilliant, a summa cum laude student at Harvard. He was a gentle soul and of a conventional mind. It would have been hard for him to deal with a wounded, temperamental, and unconventional young woman. The only memory I have of him is sliding down the gold and white curtains from the second balcony in the deserted ballroom of the Copley Plaza Hotel after the coming-out party for Ann Taylor, whose family owned the *Boston Globe*. He died the next winter in the air force.

My other beau that summer, Todd, was Irish Catholic—not my mother's choice of a young man for a supposedly well-brought-up Episcopalian daughter. Todd's father had moved his family to the North Shore when they were young,

and I had done my best to be part of their outwardly normal
family. Their daughter, Dee, was my best friend.

It wasn't rebelliousness on my part that made me fall
in love; it was the music in him, his fine voice and love of
dancing and his teasing humor. There were many other boys
that summer, but he was my star. We danced at party after
party up and down the East Coast until dawn crept across
the marble floors of the grand houses or up the golf links
of the private clubs. There were teas and luncheons and
picnics, weekends and yachts and tennis. There were long
white dresses with white gloves, and very serious marching
across the ballroom to the triumphant march from *Aida*
to curtsy to the patrons. There were long dresses in light
blues with full skirts and tightly fitted red dresses with
large balloon sleeves and soft beds in strange houses where
one woke up late with music still floating in one's ears.
It was all a dream of innocence and frivolity right out of
a musical comedy. The actors weren't quite real, as some
would remain a lifetime in that comedy, and some would
struggle to escape it. There were young men with mild
revolutionary airs and prophetic visions who danced the
nights away while declaring coming-out parties a social evil,
an inexcusable waste of money and an anachronism. While
the young men were being introduced to the lovely, well-off
girls who whirled around them, the music shot through
the night hinting that wealth and fame and power made a
difference, made it possible for things never to change, and
softly made the drama of your life more important; keep it,
keep it, was the refrain.

One night toward the end of the season, when it was
becoming apparent that the parties were going to stop soon,
Todd led me off the floor with the suggestion that we go
back to the house, change, and then go to the yacht club
to find a boat and row out into the harbor to chase the full
moon. When we got to the yacht club, the water in the bay

was black and quiet, except for the moon, which skimmed and danced on its surface—a black mirror with a blazing ball of white light. From across the harbor, we could just hear echoes of the music from the party.

Being unable to find a rowboat with oars, we simply stripped down to our underwear. I borrowed his white T-shirt and then slid off the creaking dock into the middle of the smooth, cool world of water and boats. We spent the rest of the evening swimming from boat to boat, sloop, ketch, and yacht, hauling ourselves up dripping wet over the gunnels and searching for the liquor supplies, although neither of us drank. We proceeded to imbibe whatever liquor we could find, and then collapsed on soft cushions or on the deck, discussing life, the future, friends, and serious philosophical questions. With the liquor pulling at our senses, we confused the path of the moon, slipping from boat to boat, until we were drenched with salt, the music had stopped, and the moon sank below the horizon. The day arrived with a gray and fog-bound feel to it.

That was the end of the summer, and although we didn't know it, the end of our time together and the end of the coming-out parties. I went away to college and he found other ladies. But I remember him with fondness, and think back on that night as the last real freedom of my youth, for the shadow of my mother was to grow darker.

As the coming-out parties ended, I arrived at Sarah Lawrence College, helped by my sister, who went there before me. I never discussed my going to Sarah Lawrence with my mother; I just announced I was going. She once mentioned I should go to Vassar, having no understanding that it wasn't possible—I could never have gotten in. I was a writing major and a minor in voice and psychology. Joseph Campbell was there at the time. I didn't take his course, but I read his work. "Follow your bliss," Campbell urged. I have it carved on a wooden snake over our kitchen door.

It was the beginning of an education for me. A whole new field unfolded; I could write and sing.

In psychology I started talking in class and didn't stop. We were reading a book by D. H. Lawrence, *The Man Who Died*, in which Lawrence describes in detail Christ having sexual relations. I wasn't upset about the sexual part, but Lawrence entirely missed the point of Christ's message. Christ's message was not about sex. Lawrence's book says more about Lawrence than anything else. Christ's message was spiritual, not physical.

I also took a modern dance class twice a week. It was taught by Bessie Schonberg, a very well-known and respected person in the dance world. I knew nothing about dance and I had to wear a leotard and somehow get across the floor—agony. Feeling totally uncoordinated, I would race from one side to the other as fast as possible. However, it was a start and an opening into the world of dance.

I left Sarah Lawrence College after a year. As much as I enjoyed it, I wanted to sing and be surrounded by the world of music. I applied to the New England Conservatory and, to my surprise, got in on the condition that I had to pass certain exams to become an accredited full-time student.

Opening the door to the conservatory of music was like opening a door to a life that had a reason—it was a great joy; a new family with similar interests. At last I could be free of my past. My background and my own family meant nothing to me. What mattered was that I felt I had a talent—I could sing. I had a gift to give others. I could do something in this world that would be useful, maybe even healing. I would be connected to the sounds of music, the flutes, oboes, singers, and harps. All of the instruments welcomed me, from practice rooms to Jordan Hall with its orchestra rehearsing or the opera department working on a new piece.

I perceived music as nourishment for the life of the spirit.

It coaxed and urged balance and compassion. It helped me to live in this strange world; it comforted and gave hints of other worlds, and affected me physically by calming my intense mind. I didn't know all of that when I first went to the conservatory, but I did feel very deeply the longing to make a beautiful sound with my whole body as the instrument, and eventually to express through opera all the emotions of the suicidal Carmen, the murder by Tosca, the terrible sorrow of a grandmother in Menotti's *The Consul.* My singing was fine, but my solfège, counterpoint harmony, German, Italian, and piano needed a great deal of focus.

I was happy at the conservatory and living in my paternal grandmother's house in Boston, where my mother had first seen her future husband. It never occurred to me to live with my mother. She had by now become of little consequence in my life, and to live with her certainly would have been more destructive for me, considering the unfortunate influence she already had. My future husband's grandmother lived three blocks down the avenue—they were old Boston.

Lucy was very upset that I was living with my father's mother and began circling the block and parking in front of the house, upsetting William and Atwood, my grandmother's chauffeurs. One day, I stopped my mother's little blue car and said, "I'm not leaving here and we need to get some help." To my amazement she agreed.

She kept telling the psychiatrist we went to about the poisoned milk, and he told me privately that she was a paranoid schizophrenic. Perhaps she was, but at least the psychiatrist stopped her circling the block. Years later I found myself wondering, with her rages and obsessions, if she weren't more inclined to have a borderline personality disorder, and if it could be inherited. I wondered this even more when her obsession about undulant fever and poisoned milk became even stronger, so much so that it invaded her everyday life. When I was around her, she brought out books and papers that she felt proved her point, and I wonder if perhaps at some level I felt I was full of poison. It didn't help in those years when I visited my father, when he would receive letter after letter from Lucy telling him I was not to drink the milk, as I had been very sick from it. This of course made him furious, and he would insist I drink the unpasteurized milk, especially the thick cream. I found this doubly difficult because I had never liked milk.

On the other hand, I was fortunate to have many beaux that year, and at Christmastime I was invited by one of them to go skiing in Aspen with a group from Harvard and their lady friends and mine. Among them was Bobby, six feet six inches tall, with brown hair and blue eyes. He rowed on the varsity crew at Harvard, was graduating at twenty, and had a reputation for being extremely intelligent. By chance we sat across the aisle from each other on the plane to Aspen and he talked and talked. I didn't think he was intelligent, just immensely irritating, rude, and outspoken. He talked too much. He kept following me around, and on New Year's Eve after a few drinks, he inquired into my sex life in front of all our friends gathered around the fire. After that, I did my very best to avoid him, and as I was a much better skier, I was successful. But it was a little frightening to see him plunging down the trails at great speed behind me, in a snowplow, totally out of control. On the bus back to the airport, he came and sat next to me and put his arm up behind me. I fell terribly in love on the back of the bus and married him five months later.

It hadn't really occurred to me to get married. Was it luck, karma, propinquity, or intuition to find someone I could be completely committed to and care deeply about when I was barely twenty? It was beyond my expectations. I was planning on being an opera singer.

12

Marriage and Family Ghosts

In your light I learn how to love,
In your beauty, how to write poems.
—Rumi

Bobby and I were twenty years old when we married on July 2, 1954, at the Episcopal Church in the town of Manchester-by-the-Sea, with a reception afterward at my grandfather's house. Aunt Nan had come early and fixed up the house and gardens, which were in terrible shape, with peeling wallpaper and torn curtains. Bobby had twelve ushers and I had twelve bridesmaids. We received close to three hundred presents, all of which would require thank-you notes. I wasn't particularly interested in a big wedding. I just wanted to be off with my six-foot-six, blue-eyed Irishman, as I call him; but it seemed important to everyone else. Bobby's old Boston family wasn't exactly thrilled when they heard he was marrying Sean's daughter. My father had acquired quite a reputation for being a bit of a roué, amongst other things. Bobby's uncle had been an usher at Sean and Lucy's wedding on Cumberland Island and knew him well. When Bobby told him he was marrying me, he said, "You're marrying who?" and burst out laughing.

When it came time to leave for the church, everyone drove off and left me standing in the doorway alone. When they got to the church, no one could find the bride. The church was filled and people started whispering. Bobby's father, who was an Episcopalian minister, and was to marry us, had

Bobby on his knees—Bobby said he was praying I would show up. Someone finally figured out what had happened and sent a car and I arrived at the church. My father was giving me away and, just as I was to start down the aisle, as dramatically as possible he stepped on my wedding gown so I couldn't move, but I finally reached Bobby beaming. Two of my bridesmaids wept through the entire service. It was a grand wedding; Mother stayed in the background, perhaps because Aunt Nan took over and my mother had not really played a part in my life since boarding school, but I thought she looked lovely in a long beige dress with a lace bodice and a small veil. She was delighted I was marrying Bobby because Bobby's uncle was related to the Lowells, Coolidges, Peabodys, and Gardners. Isabella Stewart Gardner left her house to the city as a museum. She was said to have scrubbed the steps of the Church of the Advent, my church with the cross, on her knees for her sins, two pet leopards in tow.

I had no interest in the fact that I was marrying into an old Boston family. I was relieved when the whole thing was over and I got in the car with Bobby.

Bobby had just missed being a Rhodes Scholar, coming in second, but he got a scholarship to Cambridge University in England. He had paid for his last two years at Harvard by working on a pipeline in Kankakee, Illinois, and Jackson, Mississippi. He wanted to pay his own way and be free of his family and his Boston ties.

We traveled all around Europe on our honeymoon and arrived at Cambridge University in the early fall. Siberian winds were already whistling through the streets. We had spent most of our money on our trip by then and had to find a flat we could afford. Our flat, on the bottom floor, had one swinging lightbulb in the living room, a tiny kitchen with a dirt floor, a nasty geyser for hot water, which I was sure was going to explode, and one "grill" heater in the bedroom, which, when huddled against, left grill marks on your skin.

It got very, very cold and I spent many days hunched over the kitchen table writing thank-you notes or taking piano lessons in mittens cut off at the fingers, or sneaking into classes in Bobby's long black robe, which I was constantly tripping over. It was a magnificent year. Bobby rowed on the Cambridge varsity crew and became a "Blue," a title of some respect in England. On vacations we traveled to Spain, Italy, Israel, and Egypt with members of the crew and other scholarship friends. One of Bobby's friends was in the Royal Air Force and flew us around in his own plane.

Toward the end of the university year, Bobby was rowing in the first boat in the Oxford-versus-Cambridge race, a big occasion in England. Mother and Jack came over with Pa, as we called my father-in-law. Jack had rowed a bit at Harvard and was thrilled about Bobby's rowing. Mother didn't have much luggage but she had brought along a very large, heavy book on brucellosis and undulant fever caused by poison milk.

I liked my in-laws. Bobby's mother was very dear and a rather typical minister's wife. In my mind Bobby's father was one of the last Puritans, craggy-faced, brilliant, a little frightening behind his Episcopalian minister's white collar. He radiated a feeling of unexplored repression as well as tremendous intelligence, and I enjoyed talks about religion with him. He was old Boston to the tightening of his skin, and the magnificent Bunker portrait we have of his mother may explain some of it. I'm sure her ramrod back never touched the back of a chair.

When I first met my father-in-law, he was serving as an interim dean at the Washington Cathedral. He had a background in engineering and they were building the cathedral. He managed, to my delight, to get the faces of a few friends and enemies carved into the gargoyles that stand guard in the cathedral towers. If you listen carefully, you can hear them laughing and see them smiling sinisterly when the cathedral bells chime out.

Bobby and I have very different temperaments in some ways. I am a woman of sorrow—"In mourning for one's life being caught in sorrow that stems from the very condition of having been born into an imperfect world," Chekhov wrote in *The Cherry Orchard*—and Bobby is a man of joy. When we got married neither of us knew I was wounded. I see the glass half empty; he sees it half full. He is intellectual and has enormous energy; I am artistic, all feelings and intuition, wanting justice (even for myself) and hating conflict. He loves to travel; I find traveling in my head much more exciting than traveling the earth with possibly less baggage. He walks into a room full of people and finds it fascinating; I walk in and cringe. I love being alone as long as Bobby is around somewhere. Neither of us has been conservative in terms of the life we've wanted to live, but we are self-referential—fortunately, both of us can spend hours alone working. He has brought the outside world to me and I have brought the inside world to him, along with the arts and the life of the spirit.

An unusual incident occurred a short time after I arrived in Boston from England ahead of Bobby. He was to finish his exams and join me. I was nine months pregnant with our first child when I moved back into my grandmother's house in Boston, claiming my old space on the third floor with a friend. My grandmother and all the help had left for Maine and the house was empty except for a dear friend who was studying at the Boston School of Art. She was a bit nervous that the child would arrive before Bobby.

The day the incident happened—and it would happen again and again—I came home rather late in the afternoon. It was hot and sultry and as I pushed open the large front door I was relieved to find the house cool. I walked through the hall and went to sit in the conservatory where there was a fountain falling into a green-and-blue-tiled pool. After cooling off in the conservatory, I went upstairs and then for some reason decided to move down to my father's bedroom on the second floor, the dreariest room in the entire house. It was large, with a high ceiling, and very dark as only Boston houses can be, with curtains that were almost black. It was really a suite with a good-sized dressing room and bathroom. Even in the middle of the day it was hard to see into the corners of this room.

The first night was fine; I slept as comfortably as someone nine months pregnant can. But the second night I woke up with the feeling that there was something or someone in the room. The room was dark and I opened my eyes slowly to see a woman in a long deep-green velvet dress and brown hair sliding in one of the windows. She fell on all fours and started crawling slowly across the room, her brown hair shifting from side to side like underwater seaweed covering her face. Her head was swinging as if she had had her throat cut or broken. Slowly she moved toward my bed, but as she got halfway there she disappeared. This happened night after night at 4:00 on the dot and woke me up. For some reason I wasn't frightened. When Bobby returned, I moved back upstairs.

My father had told me a young girl had committed suicide in that room, but I thought the apparition rather resembled Lucy—remembering when she had crawled across the floor in her long green dress toward my sister. Lucy often wore dressing gowns in the evening.

I wondered what she was trying to tell me.

Our daughter Sandra was born on July 2, 1956.

13

Children

Sandra arrived in this world with her short black hair straight up in the air and blue eyes wide open. I thought she was a miracle, sweet, warm, and beautiful. I was looking at her and still very sleepy when I noticed someone was at the end of the bed. It was my father. "It's hard to believe," he said, and I noticed there were tears in his eyes. I smiled at him and with that he turned and disappeared.

Young Angus arrived soon after Sandra. When he was born and before I saw him, Mother rushed into my room and frantically announced that Angus's umbilical cord was wrapped around his neck, strangling him. Then the doctor flew in the door and ordered her out of the hospital. Angus was fine.

Angus was a sleepy, quiet, cuddly baby. We lived in Cambridge while Bobby finished Harvard Law School and joined a law firm. I had really no idea how to bring up children—certainly not a child who turned out to have a very serious illness and whom, as it turned out, no one knew how to help.

I nursed each child for nine months. What was unsettling to me was that every time I turned over in bed to nurse Angus, Sandra would wake up and start crying. Almost every night for nine months after Angus was born, when I nursed him, she would start screaming and rocking her crib until she'd moved it all the way across her room and we had to tie it down. Bobby and I both became exhausted. Later she said there was a terrible tower in her room that went through her. I tried to keep it away by putting a favorite stuffed animal on her bed and saying it would scare away the tower. Sometimes one looks back and wishes one had done things differently, as I wish I had picked her up and taken her into our bed with Angus more when I was nursing him; but I didn't, perhaps because it would have made it hard to nurse Angus if Sandra got upset, and he was so little.

For the first five years I had the help of a lovely, calm, and sensitive older lady, Mrs. Hazlett, an experienced, dear lady, three afternoons a week. Mother had disappeared into her own life on the North Shore and Cumberland Island. When we did see her, she had no trouble with Sandra, while I had difficulty managing her. Angus continued to be a quiet child who would play by himself for hours, and if Sandra knocked him over he would just sit there and look at her. He did manage to convince me at an early age that it was the cat that "did the poopy" in his closet. I believed him.

The summer when Sandra was about five and a half and Angus was four, I took them to Northern Island, as I did every summer to be with my in-laws. Marsha, who was our babysitter for several summers, became a friend; she was half French and half Indian. (Later she became a Benedictine nun.)

Bobby would join us later. We drove up to the island, so far north near the Canadian border that we left civilization far behind. It was a sparkling late-August afternoon. From the mainland to the island was a twenty-five-minute ride in good weather. When the boat arrived, I loaded everyone on. We soon docked on the island and stepped into a scene as beautiful as a primitive painting by Grandma Moses.

The fields leading up to the houses and barns, which sat on a gentle hill overlooking the bay, sang with cicadas. The light was pristine and smooth as liquid crystal and infused with the smell of pine. On some days the island disappeared, just vanished, when all the sounds and sights were covered in a slowly rolling, thick, wet white fog.

In 1807 my husband's grandmother's grandfather's grandfather acquired Northern Island because of its unique mast
timbers (350-year-old spruce survive to this day) and the
huge tidal regimes, which could be dammed and utilized
for a sawmill and the production of barks and brigantines
for the family's merchant fleet. Only three vessels were
constructed on the island, but the family was bewitched
by the property and constructed comfortable homes, which
their descendants would visit during summer months for
the next two centuries.

The character of the place was patriarchal, as defined by
Bobby's great-grandfather, who steered the family's fortunes
from sailing ships to the American Telephone Company and
General Electric, of which his son and grandson were direc-
tors for three-quarters of the twentieth century. Although
the family was blessed with remarkable women—tales of
Isabella Stewart Gardner's efforts to provide comfort to the
hermits on Great Spruce Island made good copy for Boston's
tabloid press—the island was emphatically the province of
male energy; the main activities were fishing, hiking, and
wood-chopping. Over the years the trees grew old and
fell and new evergreens sprang up. But the island never
changed. Setting foot on it was like walking into another
dimension, into a slightly drifting world, and leaving the
old ties behind.

There were three houses on the island. Bobby's family's
home was a big yellow house reminiscent of past clipper-ship
mansions, with a wraparound porch and the most
uncomfortable furniture you could possibly imagine. Of
course, Bobby's family held that furniture as a sacred family
relic—*worshipped* it might be a better word. It was a bit of
horrible stuffed Boston, horrible stuffed seats covered with
prickly horsehair transported far to the uncivilized north.
A smaller house, called the red house, was at the bottom
of the hill and was shared by families. The third house

belonged to the patriarch's family, the Peabody Gardners (they must have intermarried a lot). This house had more charm and comfort to it, with cheerful faux painted floors and elegant stuffed furniture, portraits, good paintings, and Persian rugs.

There was also a large farm and several farmhouses run by the people who lived and worked on the island year-round, with barns for the sheep, chickens, cows, horses, and pigs. These animals provided sustenance through the cold winters, as it wasn't always possible for the people to make it to the mainland for food and supplies when the ocean froze over, so they went through the inlets that surrounded the island. In a bad snowstorm, they had to put up a rope to find their way from the farmhouse to the barn. In the summertime, there was a large vegetable garden and flower gardens.

In those days when we visited, there was still no electricity, only oil lamps. We washed all the laundry by hand on a scrub board, and used a woodstove and fireplace for heat.

On our third day there, Marsha and I decided to take the children for a picnic at one of the particularly beautiful inlets and have a dip in the icy cold water. We walked on a carpet of brown needles and outstretched roots down the trail past the chapel with its old wooden cross on the edge of the bay, surrounded by spruce trees. When we got to the inlet, we had our picnic and a dip, and then started back. It didn't take us long to realize we were lost. "Marsha," I teased, "you're part Indian. Draw on your past." "Well," she answered, "doesn't moss grow on the north side of the tree?" "Hmmm," I said, "but what direction are we supposed to be going in?" Marsha just laughed.

We have kept in touch to this day, occasionally, through letters. When she became a Benedictine nun she could never leave the abbey, where she lives now. The only way I can ever see her is through the wooden bars of the abbey reception room. She sings with the nuns about every five hours, night and day, which she loves. She wasn't altogether happy in the outside world; she is happy now. She wrote me once, "I think you and I from the first days of knowing each other, recognized in each other, that we were not of the world around us—what a long journey we've had."

We descended into trails that were very dark because the spruce and pine grew up closely together, and sometimes we had to bushwhack our way through its prickly thickness. From time to time, we would come out to huge boulders. The old Indian signs made from rock pilings didn't give us a clue about which way to go, so we went down again onto trails covered with light-green, damp, iridescent, spongy moss. It was like walking on floating green clouds.

We couldn't seem to find our way to the shore or to anything we recognized and began to believe, after about five hours, that we were going in circles. We were by now carrying the children; Angus's head was wobbling peacefully on Marsha's shoulder, and Sandra was repeatedly screaming and crying for water. Nothing Marsha or I did could stop her. I was worried that my in-laws would be getting worried. I was very fond of them both and didn't want to worry them for anything in the world. Finally we heard the large farm bell ring, and we knew then which direction to go in.

We arrived home exhausted. My in-laws were relieved to see us and didn't scold. We all went to bed early. I lay in bed in that place between sleep and wakefulness when, finally, that voice that goes on in our heads all day begins to quiet down. Then something began to bother me. Something kept seeping in on the periphery of my mind, but the uneasiness wasn't coming from the voice that spoke constantly in my head. It was more of a feeling, an impulse that finally got me out of bed. I got a flashlight and a pillow and blanket and sat down in front of the children's door. I stayed there for a minute, and then I knew very clearly why I was sitting there. Someone was trying to kidnap the children. I went to fetch an oil lamp and spent the night on the floor by their door.

The next day I mentioned to Pa, "I have this feeling that someone is thinking about kidnapping Sandra or maybe both of the children." Pa had no taste for the psychic world. He was at first surprised, thinking I might have had some real evidence, and then a bit annoyed when he discovered it was just a feeling. Pa and I talked about all sorts of things, especially religion, but we had never discussed my psychic side.

Trying to lead him in the direction I was going, I asked him about his experience with people he had been with when they died. He was thoughtful and then said, "You know, when Fletcher [his eighteen-year-old nephew] was dying from pneumonia, I was with him and just before he died he sat up in bed and said, 'Cousin George, how wonderful to see you.' Neither of us knew that Cousin George had just died."

For the next two nights, I took my blanket and lamp and lay in front of the children's door. On the second day, one of the older farmers, a large gangly man, had left the island, and no one was sure why. The next day when he didn't return, the manager went to his room. He found a letter there in which a carefully thought-out plan (conceived with his girlfriend on the mainland) was laid out. It described how they were going to kidnap Sandra at night.

14

Children's Visit to Cumberland Island

We went on an island journey in the spring of that year when Bobby and I decided we would like to go to Cumberland Island for Easter. Sandra's English godfather would fly Bobby and some friends down, and I would go on the train four days earlier with the children. I didn't want to fly with them. Mother was staying in Stafford, in the mansion house her parents moved to after Dungeness was closed. Jack had decided not to join her. It was a long journey by train from the far north to the south but exciting. We all listened to the mournful hoot of the train, sniffed the smell of burning coal, and loved the evening, rocking and rumbling through space in our berths until we felt the warm, sweet air as we reached Georgia.

We took the boat called Dungeness over to the island, and Mother greeted us on the dock. She and Sandra had a special relationship from the very beginning, and while delighted to see Sandra, she hardly paid any attention to Angus. We got in her old jitney with the cracked and broken isinglass windows, and she drove us from the dock to Stafford, which was about ten miles. The only other habitation we passed was Greyfields, the plantation house that our relatives turned into an inn and ran, and where John F. Kennedy and his bride and family stayed before their marriage years later, three miles from the dock. I had no idea who—if anyone in the family—was living on the island.

I had heard from relatives that the island was not the same and had begun to disintegrate, but I wasn't prepared for what greeted me at Stafford. The gardens had gone and the golf course was now an open rough field partly used to land small planes. The screen door was covered with "mud wamps"—wasps' nests—which made it look as if someone had thrown handfuls of mud at the door and they had grown tentacles to cling to the screen. The door was off-kilter and slightly open, and I remember thinking that Uncle Rocky had once killed a rattlesnake on the veranda by the door, and wondering if anything had slithered inside, unnoticed.

Aunt Nan and Mother had fought over the house until finally my aunt had given in. Aunt Nan had removed almost all of the furniture as part of their bargain, so the house was nearly empty, hollow and dusty. It was dusk when we walked through the door, and I remember catching sight of something out of the corner of my eye in the library that looked like a vagabond—something or someone rolled up on the floor. I didn't dare take a good look for fear it might move or groan. I later discovered that it was piles of old clothes and bedding and pillows to be thrown out. I couldn't help thinking: "Another abandoned, dust-covered house slowly decaying, this time in the moist, warm tropical air," and I felt a rush of fear and wished we hadn't come ahead of Bobby. I tried to remember if there were locks on the bedroom doors.

There was only one ship-to-shore telephone on the island and that was at the manager's house at Greyfields, some seven miles down the road. Stafford had a generator, which sometimes worked, way off in the bushes behind the house. Mother turned it on in the evenings and off when we went to bed. It gave off a kind of dim, gray light. We were alone in the house at night, and in that dim light, sitting on the steps of the terrace, I couldn't help wondering how she felt comfortable floating through her dusty spaces alone. Buhlea, one of the black people who had lived on the island all her life and knew Mother well, came during the day and fixed meals. The only time I saw Mother cry was when Buhlea died.

We ate in an empty dining room except for a long table and chairs. If Sandra got out of hand, Mother always rushed to her defense. There was an understanding, a psychic link between them that I wasn't part of, and she was quick to reprimand me. She never interfered if I scolded Angus. It sometimes made it difficult to calm Sandra down.

The rooms upstairs still had the old luxurious beds with their soft, peach monogrammed silk blanket covers and the large, old, white marble bathrooms with water that stank of sulfur, which was supposed to be good for you. The first night, the children and I slept in separate beds. I didn't sleep well. Mother slept down the hall on the other side of the house. I felt as if I were at the end of a strange world with only a worn-out jalopy to get to some kind of human contact, no key, and only candles for light.

Sandra, who knew nothing of who-whos—known by the locals as evil spirits who whispered in your ears—but carried her Scotch-Irish share of psychic ability, woke up in the deep night wailing that the who-whos were blowing in her ears. I sat next to her with my candle trying to comfort her, remembering the old stories about ghosts and who-whos—not quite able to say there are no such things as who-whos who blow in your ears; for I myself could almost hear them in the house. I took the children into my large double bed.

The second night, I heard a noise and got up, very shaken. I didn't light my candle but went to the heavy wooden door and opened it quietly. It was like the scene in *Jane Eyre* where the madwoman is locked in the attic. Mother, in her long white nightgown, candle in hand, was pushing some boxes away from the attic door. When she finished, she drifted up the attic stairs and disappeared. I went to bed that night feeling very unsettled. I felt bad for my mother. She must have been puzzled and disappointed, but I left with the children the next day.

15

Suicide

Though our trip to Cumberland Island had been unsuccessful, I still went to their house on the North Shore on occasion to visit Mother and Grand Jack, as we called him, so she could see the children. I believe in some way I still felt I needed to take care of her. They had been married five years. We drove up one Sunday from Cambridge with the children. Mother refused to set foot on Crescent Island—where father now lived with his second wife and three children. They were still living in Grandfather Carnegie's old large house where Bobby and I were married. This house, too, was slowly decaying.

When Jack moved in, the house had already begun to disintegrate—peeling wallpaper, torn screens, and tattered curtains. I often wondered what Jack ate, as he always complained that he could never find Mother. She often disappeared, and he suspected she was in the attic.

Mother continued to adore Sandra and it was fascinating to see them together, as if they shared a secret bond none of the rest of us understood. She still ignored Angus. She would take Sandra for a walk in what was left of the garden and Sandra never seemed to cause a problem around her. Mother made Sandra a long snake like toy out of bits of colored cloth, which Sandra adored. It wasn't very well put together, and when it got pulled apart by accident one day, Sandra completely lost control. She remembered that snake well into her adulthood.

Jack was especially fond of Bobby because of Bobby's noteworthy rowing achievements, and we were both fond of

Jack—he was a sweet and gentle soul. The last time we went to visit, the children were six and four and a half. He met us at the door, and if either of us had known then what we know now, we might have been able to help. We did know he had been in and out of McLean Hospital for depression, or manic depression as they called it, but we really didn't understand what that meant or the possible consequences. His face was pale and his eyes were frighteningly dead— almost as if he couldn't see us.

He kept jumping up at lunch and singing his favorite song, "Me and My Shadow," and twirling an imaginary cane and taking off and putting on again an imaginary top hat. Wildly waving his hands up and down, he complained, "Your mother pushes me down then pulls me up. Then she disappears into the attic." After lunch he fell into a deep sleep on the sofa. We left shortly afterward. We didn't understand that his sleeping was a sign of depression—he never drank. He said something to Sandra, who was six at the time, that appeared to bother her. "He kept saying good-bye," she said when Bobby and I questioned her.

Old Great Aunt Bebe—Grandmother's youngest sister, who lived up the hill nearby, where Jack and Mother were married—would often send Mrs. Gwin, a cook from the village, to fix a meal and let Aunt Bebe know how things were. I sat there wondering what Mrs. Gwin was thinking.

Jack's simple mind was being slowly eroded and he had no defenses. Lucy had a very strong, obsessive, sick view of reality and she played the themes of poison milk over and over, and by then, Cumberland Island had become another serious obsession as the federal government was slowly taking it over. She hired lawyers and went to court; papers and letters about Cumberland littered the house.

*

Several weeks later, just after coming back from a singing lesson, I got a message from our housekeeper that we should go to Mother's immediately—something had happened to Jack. When we got there and started up the driveway, I had a sense of foreboding. We opened the front door to find policemen and private detectives in the house. They didn't mince words: Jack was dead from a shotgun wound that blew off his head. They were questioning my mother—for murder. This was, I learned, routine in such cases. I don't believe anyone thought that Mother had anything to do with the actual suicide.

After an extensive investigation, it was determined that Jack had committed suicide. He had held the trigger with his toe and shot himself in Grandmother's bed, surrounded by stacks of papers and big old black books on the bureau, floor, bed—papers about poison milk, about Cumberland Island. A paper epitaph.

Mother would never believe he killed himself; it was an intruder, she insisted. Some said no one could live with Mother; it was the second suicide in an empty house.

When I went over to touch Mother the day Jack was shot, she felt cold as ice. I don't believe the investigation bothered her. She said in a whisper, "How could Jack do this to me?" I don't remember that we ever spoke of what happened. Mother moved to a smaller house and saw less and less of her family.

I learned before the funeral that the Episcopalian and Catholic churches did not accept Jack's suicide. They believed that those who committed suicide could not go to Heaven. I was furious—those who believe such things know nothing of pain, mental pain, which is sometimes worse than physical pain. I prayed that Jack would get into Heaven before all of them and welcome them with his gentle spirit and his little song-and-dance number, "Me and My Shadow."

16

Sandra and Psychiatrists

I enrolled both children when they were four and five-and-a-half in a little Episcopalian nuns' school about three blocks from us in Cambridge, and it was then that I had the first inkling that something was wrong with Sandra. Sister Natalie, a dear nun, asked to meet with me. Looking very uncomfortable, she said, "Something is not quite right with Sandra. We can't relate to her. She's unhappy and has problems with the other children. We have a hard time controlling her. Angus is just fine and a dear happy child." That was the beginning. I had no idea that the way Sandra behaved wasn't normal.

After law school, Bobby wanted to take some time off and travel. We left the children with Bob's parents and a trained children's nurse who had helped bring up my half brothers and sisters. Sandra was very unhappy that we had left her; she was out of control, according to the nurse, who said she'd never had such a difficult child. After our talk, I began to wonder what was wrong. Was it something I was doing? I felt I really didn't know how to be a mother, given my life and experience with my own mother. Should we not have left her alone at such an early age? But that's what people did in those days.

At six Sandra moved on to a progressive school in Cambridge, and one day I got a call from the first-grade teacher, who was popular with the children. "Something is not working for Sandra. We can't control her, the work is very hard for her, and she has trouble getting along with other children. She keeps hiding in the bathroom and disrupting the class. Could we talk?" They wanted me to meet with the school psychiatrist. I was appalled. What if my daughter was ill like Lucy?

The psychiatrist at the school suggested that Sandra and I both go to the Jackson Clinic in Jamaica Plain, a well-known clinic for children just outside of Boston. I could see the male psychiatrist who was head of the clinic while Sandra saw a female child psychiatrist. At that time, women for the most part didn't work; they stayed home and took care of the children—so the mother was more likely to be held responsible.

I found it difficult to talk to my psychiatrist; I wasn't used to talking about myself. Also, without anyone directly saying anything, I felt accused of being responsible for Sandra's problem. They hadn't suggested Bobby see anyone. It appeared the mother was the problem.

After about a year, my psychiatrist started canceling appointments or changing the time. I was beginning to get depressed by the situation, which didn't help my growing problems with Sandra. At one session I told him that I had started to faint in the car while driving down Storrow Drive. He said, "You don't know what it's like to faint." I was discouraged. It was a warning signal that my therapy was going nowhere. Something was wrong and nothing I was doing there was helping with Sandra. She still would get very angry and scream and yell until she was totally out of control. If anything, her condition was getting worse.

Bobby received a call from a friend of ours on the board of the clinic, who said that my psychiatrist was being relieved of his position at the clinic and probably his entitlement to practice. His patients were becoming suicidal and depressed. I went to see him one last time, as the clinic said there should be some kind of closure. I don't remember what he said, but I suddenly had a hallucination of a mass of blood and gore, and got up and fled from the room.

It was a terrible time for Bobby and me, as my being depressed made it even more difficult. I just wanted to shut my door and be alone for weeks on end and didn't understand why. This drove Sandra to distraction and she would bang on the door, yell and scream. Bobby did what he could, and so did our housekeeper, but she couldn't help either. We had followed the psychiatrists' advice, visited her at the hospital, gone into family therapy—all to no avail. My psychiatrist, who also saw Bobby from time to time, said we shouldn't have any more children and should probably get a divorce.

Sandra was so easily frustrated. If she couldn't reach a bottle on a high shelf at the grocery store, she would burst out screaming; and once she started, there was no stopping it. Over and over, she said, "You don't love me." She was a beautiful child, but her face often radiated anger. Night after night, Sandra would disrupt dinner so no one could talk. She would say, "Why are you talking to Angus? Stop it." Then she would grab the dinner knife and start to make holes in the table. I would get up and take her upstairs to calm her down. She wouldn't stay and would come back down, often screaming. I felt utterly hopeless—I couldn't stop her. I blamed myself.

Bobby and I felt overwhelmed. We didn't know what to do to help our child. Sandra was flying into rages that I couldn't stop. It became impossible to discipline her. Guilt settled in and became a constant companion for us.

Then Sandra went over the line one day and let our chow dog, Kubie, out of the backyard—undoing the knot was strictly forbidden because he could easily be killed by the traffic at the end of the street. I ran after him and found him sitting in the middle of three-way traffic. When I got Kubie home, I went to my room and tried to think through what had happened. I came to the conclusion that this situation was far more serious than we understood.

Many years later, Sandra sued for all the doctors' reports. Her psychiatrist had written: "Sandra's focus is her desperate struggle with her brother over her mother's attention. The mother is a vacant vain person who is self preoccupied and has little to give her children."

It was a good thing I didn't see their report at the time, but I got the message: *You, the mother, are full of poison and were yourself unwanted. How could you love and care for a daughter?*

Singing

The eyes of the skull in the corner of Eric Schroeder's window blinked in the shadow of the candle he kept next to it to shed light on his charts. Two bald heads bent intent on the task in front of them as they puzzled out the old maxim, "As above, so below" and charted the dance of the Ram and Scorpion, all the animals of the zodiac making their way through the shadows of the night. Schroeder, the keeper of Islamic Art at the Fogg Museum, had written the definitive book on Islamic civilization, called *Muhammad's People*. It was rumored that he had been to Mecca, had a continuing fascination and a love affair with death, and had spent some thirty years plotting the skies and the ways of man with his horoscopes.

I found his presence across the street comforting, and I watched him at night from our upstairs window, curious. "It was a dream," he said, that brought him across the street to knock on my door. "I would like to do your horoscope. I dreamed about you and Sandra and your mother. I am particularly interested in those relationships."

I turned away and didn't answer for a moment. Our daughter, now eight, was clearly not well. Somehow I was not in the least surprised to find Eric on our doorstep asking such a question. The world of the psyche had been mine since birth. In fact, it was sometimes more real to me than what everyone knew as the real world, but I was in awe and fear of it. I believed in many things I never spoke about and tried to keep clear of the psychic world, afraid that it might pull me over into an unsettled mind. I seldom visited it;

however, it often knocked at my door.

All these thoughts were racing through my head as I turned back to Eric and looked straight at him as I calculated the consequences, then murmured, "All right." Eric, never having set foot in the house, turned and left.

Two weeks later I stood by his desk, a nervous quality about me like a bird, as if I were ready to take flight if necessary, as if some imprint or haunting from my past made me fear banishment or instant annihilation, a dreamer and a singer with raw energy and a desperate need to be alone much of the time. I believed that symbols were reality, that thoughts were as powerful as actions and had consequences, and that I should save those I loved. Standing beside Professor Schroeder, I took in every word he said (and it affected the rest of my life) at some deep level not entirely consciously, and I began to make a connection between Sandra and Mother.

"A Libra, with a Scorpio mother and a Cancer daughter. A Libra," he said, "with hardly any earth signs and a great deal of water in your chart, perhaps too much, makes you extremely sensitive, which can lead to penetrating intuition or overreacting to the slightest stimulus. One can become devitalized by fear, worn out, prompting you to withdraw to an inner life."

Then Eric, small and quick, a man of few words who hadn't even invited me to sit, turned and looked at me, and said, "You will not be a singer; a few small concerts here and there and that is all."

My eyes fell to the floor not soon enough to hide the terror; I was just starting a singing career, just beginning to turn professional. I had been accepted in the soloist department at Tanglewood for the summer. My whole hope of life was in my singing.

"Your myth," he continued, "is the myth of Orpheus. You know everyone has a myth. If you understand your myth you will understand a great deal about yourself. There are several versions of this myth. Your version is the one in which Orpheus is torn apart by women. His head is thrown into the river where it recites poetry and prophesies. He was a priest and a shaman—he descends into the underworld."

"Orpheus was a singer and a man," I said in almost a whisper. Eric nodded, and that was the end of our meeting. I crossed the street and stood stunned by my front door; I felt ill. Orpheus enchanted the very birds with his singing, but he goes to the underworld—I shivered—and is torn apart by women. It wasn't until years later, when remembering that my myth was the myth of Orpheus that the concept began to form in my mind—I would feel torn apart by the two women closest to me, then they would fade away like Eurydice. The gift of prophecy would come and go, and my writing would have a touch of poetry about it, but I would only sing when released by the Gods to sing amongst the stars. (Orpheus lost the feminine—long ago I learned much of the role of Orpheus in the opera *Orpheus and Eurydice*. I sang Orpheus because it was often sung by a mezzo.)

I decided to go to the opera department at Boston University. It was 1964 and the children were both in grade school.

I had started singing around town, performing leading roles in Menotti's *The Consul* and *Amahl and the Night Visitors*. When I went to BU, Sarah Caldwell, director of the opera department, was becoming a famous opera impresario; she would eventually end up on the cover of *Time* magazine. I got small parts and chorus parts in *Susannah*, *Gianni Schicchi*, and *Madame Butterfly*. I also auditioned for Caldwell's professional company, where I sang in the chorus with stars from the Metropolitan Opera. I sang in choirs and performed leads in summer stock—five lines as a prostitute in *The Ballad of Baby Doe* with the New York City Opera when it came to Boston—and Handel solos on

Channel Two. Best of all, I auditioned for the conductor of the Boston Symphony and was accepted to the soloist department at Tanglewood. I remember my amazement when the well-known head of the choral department at the New England Conservatory rushed up to me after the audition in which I sang "Stride la Vampa" ("Burn the Witch") and grabbed my hand. I was hoarse that day and surprised the audition went so well. But I never got to Tanglewood.

It happened slowly. Sometimes I couldn't talk and some days I was a little flat, and then it just got worse and worse and I started losing my voice altogether. Exams came and I tried to walk up the wide white marble steps to where the exams were being given. The stairs swam under my feet. I clung to the railing. The staff on the blackboard I needed to copy merged on my paper into a tangle of lines. I couldn't sing for the exams—I tried but I panicked and I felt the old inability to function starting again. I got a letter one day from the head of the department saying I had to leave BU. I was devastated. For fifteen years afterward I could not listen to opera, Mahler, Brahms, or Schubert. Only once in the next thirty years did I sing. It didn't really occur to me then that this might have had something to do with my mother. If one is not cared for or doesn't feel loved, one doesn't understand the consequences or how others are able to function comfortably in the world. But now I see the connection: I had lost my voice as a child, so I had lost it again as a woman.

One summer when Bobby and his cousin and I were up at Northern Island, enjoying the peace and quiet beauty of the place, I was sitting in the large, sun-drenched kitchen. The radio was on. The singer must have been a young boy whose voice had not yet changed. I was writing in my journal when it drifted through the room. The purest voice I ever heard—the voice of an angel. He was singing "Panis Angelicus," a plea for help. "Father, father keep us within your care." I found myself standing up to pay better attention and then felt the pain pour from the roots of my hair down to the soles of my feet. I got up and put on *Amahl and the Night Visitors*, in which I had once sung the lead, the part of the mother. I started to sing without any thought, just feeling moved by the music and the story. I remembered it all and sang it in full voice, high notes floating out to a quick crescendo. Bobby and his cousin came out of the library to listen. It all just floated out of me, out of the open windows across the fields to the bay. The story is about Amahl, a young boy, and his mother, who are very poor and hungry. The Three Kings (in the Bible) are on their way to visit the Christ child and stop by for shelter. In the end, Amahl goes with them:

AMAHL: "So my darling, goodbye. I shall miss you very much."

MOTHER: "I shall miss you very, very much! Don't forget to wear your hat."

AMAHL: "Yes, I promise. Feed my bird."

MOTHER: "Yes, I promise. I shall miss you very much."

I tried again the next day. I couldn't sing. I had wanted to celebrate life by singing. It had been my way out— rich or poor. It was how I would be a person in my own right; through my voice I would be heard and seen. I had to find other ways to celebrate life, but they would never fulfill the longing as singing had. Nothing ever again offered me such a direct, enchanting, and amazing path to the spiritual world. Nothing ever eased that longing either.

"God admires me when I work, but loves me when I sing." How I longed for that love through singing.

I heard that Sarah Caldwell said that I had one of the best nonprofessional voices she had ever heard. In a rehearsal of

Othello, I sang in her professional chorus and Tito Gobbi grabbed my hat from my hand and pulled it down over my eyes, laughing because I didn't know I was supposed to wear the hat the way the costume designer had indicated, and had gotten in trouble in the rehearsal. Years later I had an opportunity to talk with Sarah, and she asked me why I stopped singing. I quoted Callas: "Happy birds sing, unhappy birds don't."

Sandra, who has one of the loveliest, most haunting voices I have ever heard, and who wanted to sing, not opera but folk songs, had the same fate, or perhaps just stopped.

I am still not sure why I lost my voice. I thought maybe it was the past, maybe Sandra becoming sicker, and the growing chaos at home. I was never to sing again.

18

Eminent Domain

Not long before she died, Mother told me I would inherit a tract of land beside the small beach house on Cumberland Island. We added a kitchen, bunk beds for the children, a room for ourselves, and a small leaky pool and deck. The beach house was the only house that was left intact and livable on the twenty miles of beach. When we went back in the hot summertime, Sandra was at camp, and I would wake up very early, get in our jeep, and drive down the wide, hard sand beach for miles, loving the cooling wind. I'd stop the car and strip and swim in the warm, probably dangerous ocean. Then, salt-licked and sticky, I would drive back. At the time after Mother's death, I also inherited all the problems and heartaches that went with the island.

Some of the Carnegie relatives needed money, and some of them wanted very much to keep the island. Perhaps the relatives who wanted to sell had more incentive and drive and organization than those who wanted to keep it. In any case, those who wanted to sell had gone to the federal government and Andrew Mellon with their plan. The Andrew Mellon Foundation, run by my former Grove Hall roommate's family, put up the money for the National Park Service to start buying the island, and they now owned about 70 percent of it. The crushing part was that those of us who didn't want to sell found our land would be condemned. That meant the land was taken by eminent domain and the money given to the owners. How much is something worth if you don't want to sell it?

This happened in the 1960s, when the federal government had funds and there was a great hue and cry to save the wilderness. I was never against preserving the wilderness, but I could not understand how they could take away our land and homes. Didn't I have any rights at all to my property, to my swing and my view of the ocean?

I went back to the island once after the Park Service took control—there are still several relatives who have kept houses for their lifetimes. Greyfields has become an inn run by the family. Plum Orchard, taken over by the Park, has become run-down and deserted. My niece and sister held on to Stafford, where our grandparents ended up living, because the Park Service ran out of funds, and I was allowed to keep my beach house for fifteen years.

In the 1960s there was a man with sandy hair who often went to Cumberland Island. Sometimes he stopped at the little beach house that Mother had given to me and swung on my swing overlooking the dunes and the sea.

It was that sandy-haired man, the one who rocked on my swing, who would determine much of the fate of Cumberland Island. He was Jimmy Carter, who became governor of Georgia at the time when the federal government and the Mellon Foundation were trying to take over the island. Bobby was running for the U.S. Senate in Maine and trying to do everything he could to hold on to my Cumberland Island property. If we were forced to sell and lose the beach house (they told my sister they would put a lock on her door if she didn't comply), then at least we would get top value. Our side was hard to defend, as there was great public support for taking private wilderness.

Bobby and I and a young man who worked with Bobby got on a plane and went down to visit Governor Carter in Georgia. Bobby was told not to speak very much, as he was always outspoken, and it was assumed that I wouldn't say much; our young friend, who was not a lawyer, was to do most of the talking. In the meeting, I was furious as I sat there listening and finally exclaimed, "How would you like it if someone came along and took your peanut farm in Georgia?" I don't remember the rest of the conversation; I just remember that Carter smiled a lot.

A few years later, when Carter was president of the United States, we ended up at a cocktail party together in Washington, D.C. I looked across the room and there he was, smiling at me. He walked across the room with Rosalynn trailing behind and gave me a kiss. Rosalynn, looking very cross, turned on her heel and stalked away.

"Well," I said to the president, "you got it, didn't you, swing and all?"

19

Curbstone

*If in the twilight of memory should we meet once more,
we shall speak again together and you shall sing me a deeper
song.* —Khalil Gibran

When Mother was in her sixties she moved to the island.
The island was her one refuge, except for a few months
of the summer spent on the North Shore of Boston. Just
before I inherited the beach house and the incident with
President Carter, Lucy left Stafford Plantation and moved
to a little house with a pool just down the road, called the
Chimneys. The house was called that because the chimneys
were left still standing where slaves had once lived. Stafford
had grown dilapidated to the point where she couldn't live
there. In her old age, she lived amongst the remaining
chimneys of the old slave quarters of the five hundred slaves
that Robert Stafford had owned on his plantation before
the Civil War. The Sicilian donkeys, now wild, still woke
her up in the morning and the palm trees rustled, and she
killed water moccasins that slithered out of the pool with
a hoe. The Spanish moss, like a dead man's beard, grew in
the trees and strangled them until they became bone white.
The avenue of trees going up the road to Stafford died after
spreading their gnarled roots across the road and opening up their bare, skinny branches for the black buzzards
and vultures. The ghosts of the slaves and spirits rattled
through the palmettos at night but Mother felt at one with
them. Nate, a black gentleman who grew up on the island,
moved into the little servants' quarters and cared for her.
He drank a bit and sang and talked to his pots and pans a
great deal—but it was fine because he and Lucy understood

talking to the pots. No other person had ever been able to care for Lucy besides Nate. She was quite ill with bone and stomach cancer. I think my mother would have preferred to die there on her island, but it wasn't to be.

I couldn't in good conscience not take her to the Massachusetts General Hospital. I flew down in a small plane with a pilot who was a friend of ours to pick Mother up. We managed to land on the bumpy field at Cumberland after several attempts at scaring Aunt Fergie's cows off the so-called runway. It was late spring and the southern air was warm. Mother said she had been happy on the island with Nate.

She needed medical attention badly, and no one had been able to persuade her to come north. Her stomach was distended until she looked nine months pregnant, and she was getting weak. She carried on a little about being poisoned by "the milk," but only halfheartedly. I asked her if she was afraid, and she said no. We never seemed able to talk much to each other. There was no connection; there was nothing to which I could attach.

When we arrived in Boston, we went to a hotel on Beacon Street, the center of the old Boston world. The next day I was taking her to the hospital. We walked out onto Beacon Street to get the car. Mother was dressed in a maternity dress with gay pink flowers on it. She was carrying a rubber bridge table mat and two rolls of toilet paper, and wearing a shower cap and winter boots lined with wool. It was June. She walked a little way and stopped. Then Lucy Carnegie spread the mat on the curbstone on that eminent Boston street and sat down. I watched her for a moment, and when I realized she wasn't going to move, I sat down beside her. We looked at each other, and both of us began to giggle. It was probably the closest we ever got.

Mother died soon after. In the last month, she refused to see anyone but me. The night she died she said, "Millicent, is that you! I'm so glad you're here." I rocked her in my arms, gently toward her death.

She left me a personal treasured gift, a box with six knives with mother-of-pearl handles and a note inside:

To my daughter, good and kind,
who always cared for me and
was never behind my back.

Andrew and Thomas Carnegie (my great-grandfather) as children.
Thomas is the younger boy.

My great-grandfather Thomas Morrison Carnegie and my grand-father, Andrew Carnegie II, a dear and kind man with whom I spent several summers and frequent winter visits at the Ritz Hotel in Boston.

Lucy Carnegie and her nine children. Andrew Carnegie II (my grandfather) is in the center in front of Mama Negie.

The main road is fifteen miles long on Cumberland Island, with a white, oyster-shell surface. This photo was taken many years ago when the roads were kept up.

A typical family gathering at Dungeness. This picture shows Grandma Negie and many of her nine children.

My grandmother Bertha Sherlock Carnegie (center) with
Aunt Nan (left) and Mother (right). Lucy was probably three
years old when this photograph was taken.

My mother, Lucy Coleman Carnegie, in her teens.

Lucy in front of Dungeness.

Mother on her wedding day, surrounded by bridesmaids.

Lucy on her wedding day. Sean and Lucy were married at
Dungeness in 1924.

Mother was an accomplished rider and a great shot.
Because of this, her father called her Bill.

Mother has just shot a turkey.

Aunt Nan and Uncle Rocky on a shooting expedition in the 1950s.

Bobby rowing for Cambridge University at Putney Bridge in 1955. He rowed number 6 in the boat race and was awarded a "Blue."

This portrait was painted by Georgia Augusta and hangs in our living room.

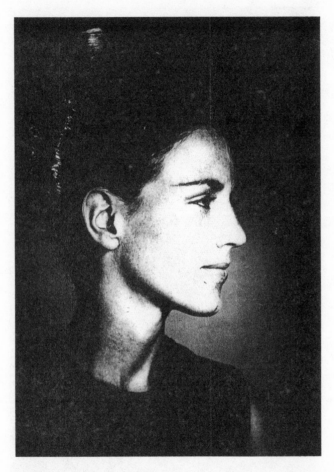

This photograph of me was taken when I was auditioning for summer stock and opera in Boston in my twenties and thirties.

I can see these two views from the room I call my tower, where I write. Their moods and beauty provide comfort and inspiration and remind me often to be thankful for so much beauty.

The North Island, showing its bays and outer islands. There is a beauty and charm in this place, basically uninhabited except for the farmhouse, a few family houses, and the north wind.

This picture of our children, Angus and Sandra, was taken during a family holiday on the North Island.

The dock and two of the family houses on the North Island.

Andrew Carnegie with his daughter, Aunt Nan, and nieces and nephews.

Part Two

20

Crescent Island— Middle Island

Then there is the middle island, Crescent Island, the island of two rivers, the Sedego and Crescent. These rivers form its boundaries, running through the saltwater marshes to the dunes, the beaches, and the ocean. The middle island touches on the edge of the North Country off the coast of Maine, and a cold sea forms its boundaries to the east. It is connected to the mainland and to the community by the Aulde Bridge. This is the island of relationships, work and family. This middle island belonged to my paternal ancestors.

In the 1890s my great-grandfather D. W., my father's grandfather, was taking the train from Boston along the coast of Maine to go hunting with some friends. Looking out the window, he saw land that intrigued him. He got up, pulled the cord to make the train stop (you could in those days), left his companions, and began walking. What he saw was land of immense beauty: beaches, dunes, islands, rivers, fields, and rich woodland. Over the ensuing years he bought up property little by little from the farmers until he had three thousand acres. He called it Crescent Island as it was surrounded by water on three sides.

D. W. first fixed up an old house called the gun cottage overlooking the ocean. Then he built houses for the farmers, a horse barn that was run by a groom, Mr. Adkins, and his daughter, and planted a glorious garden by the sea that had large oval iron cages containing green, yellow, and orange parrots; they made a dreadful racket. He built three good-sized greenhouses and a duck shoot for hunting, filled the fields with corn, hay, and vegetables, and built a huge barn to store hay and a good-sized cow barn for a bull and thirty cows that provided the family with milk. I can still remember, when I was about five or six, the sweet sickly smell of fresh, white, unpasteurized milk being poured warm and bubbling into the huge vat to be distributed into bottles. I remember my grandfather with his white pointed beard and dignified manner feeding the deer that he had penned for many acres.

When great-grandfather D. W. died, he left Crescent Island to his son, who in turn left it to my father. In the late 1930s, just before World War II, he built a solid, sprawling new house of gray stone and wood. When he returned from World War II, he settled on Crescent Island and created a corporation in which all of his children and stepchildren (which in the end turned out to be eight of us) could have long-term rentals, but no one could own the land or sell it; a family corporation was to run it. There are now some forty of us on the island year-round, and that swells to about sixty in the summer with children and grandchildren. The younger generation runs the corporation now and holds it firmly and kindly in their hands.

Crescent Island's ocean shore faces to the east. Five beaches rim its perimeter; two beaches look directly out to sea to a long stretch of blue horizon. Another beach faces a long island called Cove Island. The west beach borders on an estuary where the Periwinkle River runs over long clam flats to the sea. The water is clean in the inlets where one can see the brown underwater seaweed moving in slow motion with the tide.

A breakwater to Cove Island, built many years ago, makes a harbor between the mainland and the island and creates a bay. Cove Island is about two miles long and deserted except for an old log cabin. On either side spruce trees grow and in the middle is a long, gentle stretch of fields.

On Crescent Island there is a hill filled with blueberries overlooking the river; the property has ducks, deer, raccoons, wild turkeys, quail, rabbits, skunks, coyotes, and blue herons, as well as an occasional moose or mountain lion. Flocks of geese visit in the fall.

Foxes breed in the dunes in the spring: the mother nurses her young on the dunes' edge against a backdrop of the sea, and the father, when their bellies are full, walks the little balls of fur in a line behind him down the sea path. Muskrats loll in the sun, porcupines make their meal by destroying the trees, and owls make their evening dinner of small creatures. The morning dove coos sadly at daybreak; in the warm weather, monarch butterflies add wings to flowers; deer stand dead still before leaping into the forest or race in herds down the beach before sunrise for a swim; moose stand knee-deep in ponds; and the coyotes howl at night as the wildcats wait.

The Periwinkle and Sedoc rivers form the island's boundaries, running through the saltwater marshes and wetlands to the sea. They are joined by the Aulde Bridge at Crescent Field, which connects the island to the mainland. A hidden pond in the winter, a mile into the woods, freezes over with smooth, blue ice for skating.

This island's spell is its ocean, pushing and pulling at its perimeter. Its sound murmurs or roars through the forest, and the wind whips across the water carrying the heavy smell of salt and seaweed while the moon tugs beneath the surfaces of huge tides pulling at the earth's circumference.

On this island it's hard to escape the ocean's roaring waves, coastal winds, or foaming fury, sending spray a quarter of a mile ashore to kill the pines, or its soft lapping at the beaches. In the months of bitter cold, when the waves break they sound like shards of broken crystal, and when it's silky calm the early morning light shines on the water's surface. Then a thousand gaily colored buoys, unseen before, mysteriously appear back-lit and float to be collected by the lobster boats, while large flocks of birds skim across the surface and seagulls scream, cry, and laugh all day, swinging from the sky. Ospreys with long, fierce claws clasped around the belly of a fish make loud, ghastly screeching sounds while devouring their silent prey, and bald eagles silhouetted against black rocks sit patiently.

On days when there is a mist over the island, the sea grass drips with crystal pearls, and when the fog envelops everything, one can hear the bell buoy and the groaner singing their strange duet all across the dunes.

We moved to Crescent Island to bring up our family when the children were in their early teens. Crescent Island was to be where Sandra would live when she became an adult.

21

Sandra
(Ages Ten to Fifteen)

From the age of around ten to thirteen, Sandra seemed to improve, and things went better for all of us. It felt cyclical—there would be fairly good periods and then things would fall apart. She went to camp for two summers with two cousins. We bought her a horse called Peter that she took to camp, and she won a blue ribbon. There were problems, but she seemed to enjoy camp. According to her report: "She was in three plays and had an excellent sense for skits, got good reports on her riding and swimming, and loved sailing, did not care for tutoring." Her counselor's comments were: "She showed only occasional respect for authority, she is a child of opposites, moody and unpredictable at most moments, extremely sensitive and easily hurt, other times she is tough as nails, sometimes cute and funny, other times belligerent and rebellious." The head of the camp said, "If Sandra gets more control of herself, we would love to see her in camp next year."

We moved her to a new school in Cambridge, which appeared to be working a bit better for her. She was told she could go a long way on the parallel bars. She had a good friend there named Alice, who, we learned from the teacher, was quite troubled. Bobby's niece had come to live with us so she could go to school in Boston (which turned out to be helpful for Sandra), and so did Elk, Bobby's cousin, a former bass player. They lived on the third floor and Sandra spent a lot of time up there with them, but still life around Sandra, especially for Bobby and me, was exhausting. We would get into useless arguments about what to do, arriving at no solution. Sometimes Sandra would accuse me of being angry when I wasn't—usually it was when she was about to fly into a rage. I couldn't have expressed it then but her tantrums felt like an invasion of my very being that I couldn't control or stop.

We spent every summer and several vacations on Crescent Island after the children turned eleven and twelve, in a ramshackle house on the edge of the sea, flanked by dunes and a long, curved beach, with an island making a bay on one side and the open ocean on the other. By then Bobby's niece had left us, but my two nephews, who were about Angus's age, joined us. Bobby's sister and her five children moved in next door.

We were very fortunate that the McPhees, Dot and Phil, came down from Canada to join us on Crescent Island. I'm not sure how we would have managed without them. Phil was a retired policeman, which turned out to be a blessing. Bobby, when Angus got old enough, bought him an old lobster boat, and Angus started a small lobster business with various cousins. I can still see him at the wheel of that boat just at dawn, heading off to sea by himself. Like me, he has always needed to be alone.

When Sandra was twelve I started a summer theater on Crescent Island in our family's large barn. The third year it became an equity theater, and at the end of the fifth year I closed it and started a modern dance company. Sandra took part in the theater for two summers and really enjoyed it. She played the young girl as the lead in *The Potting Shed* as well as bit parts in the musicals we put on. She was a good, natural actress and loved being around the theater and other actors.

Things at home in Cambridge in the winter of Sandra's fourteenth year did not go well; she was getting totally out of hand. That was the year the hippies moved into Cambridge. They set up camp in the park right near us and Sandra started hanging around with them. We were naïve and didn't realize that Sandra had gotten into dope and drinking.

Bobby and I were desperate and exhausted, which only made matters worse. We were pouring all our emotional resources into just trying to survive at the moment when she needed us most. We had a long talk one evening, and decided we were getting no help, nor was Sandra, from the professionals. She was refusing to talk to her psychiatrist, and the report from a psychologist who tested her told us he had no idea how we lived with the amount of rage that Sandra was feeling and acting out. We had to do something.

Bobby made arrangements for Sandra to go to a private school in Switzerland. It may not have been the right thing to do, but we didn't want to institutionalize her, and there didn't appear to be any appropriate boarding school here. He flew over with her to make sure the school was a good place for her. For Christmas, Bobby, Angus, and I flew over to pick up Sandra and we all went on a safari. The incredible beauty of Africa spoke to all of us, but the trip was pretty miserable because Sandra got so upset, refusing to go where we had planned, upsetting the guide, and tormenting Angus verbally.

When Sandra went back to school, she decided she wanted to go to McLean Hospital—famously memorialized by Robert Lowell in his poem "Waking in the Blue" as "the house for the 'mentally ill'" (the quote marks indicate Lowell's own skepticism of the term's credibility). Sandra claimed it was because her friend Donna was there, as was a famous singer. She was ready to give up the struggle. She begged the psychiatrist she'd seen in Switzerland to write a letter saying she needed hospitalization. Bobby, a man accustomed to success and to solving problems with a focused effort, experienced the progressive horror of his daughter drifting to a shore he could not access, his immediate family shattered by the insistence of her illness and his beloved wife tormented by the felt accusation of others that she was somehow responsible. An innocent, he adapted rapidly to the realities of mental illness—the array of professionals, earnest and without self-doubt, the bewildering variety of possible treatments. During a Christmas stay at a treatment center—informed by the "wisdom" of profoundly self-confident "healers"—Bobby sat down and wrote a letter to his daughter for her to read when she came home:

Dear Sandra,

As I look out of the glass door overlooking the dunes and ocean a deep sadness pervades my being as I think of you.

I can understand your mind in its impatient brilliance. It is the great excitement of my life to be your father. This I know, but I also know the pain of feeling utterly unable to convince you that I love you and want to help or that you can TRUST me.

It has taken me a long time to get to this point of acknowledging the pain. I feel the pain of not having a "family" in the sense that I wanted one—a unit of people whose feelings towards each other and interacting supportiveness make each as much as they can be. It is perhaps the sense of personal failure that is the most painful to me, although there is great pain in thinking (as I often do) of the beautiful talented girl who is my daughter, with so much to give, but so much difficulty in maintaining relationships with people who need and would welcome what she has to give.

The first thought I had of you was on 1 July 1954, the day before I got married. I was walking through downtown Manchester by the sea with Austin Higgins, my brother-in-law, best man and lifelong friend.

*I asked him about the advisability of having chil-
dren early in marriage—he replied with quick and
affectionate bewilderment that children were what it
was all about. Then, I knew that I would try to have
children right away. Your mother was agreeable; you
were conceived in love as our very much wanted child.
You began to arrive at the Boston Lying-in Hospital
where you appeared shortly before noon on June 26th,
1956.*

*I have long thought about our inexperience and
how it might have adversely affected you. Certainly,
over the years, various psychologists gave expert focus
on our deficiencies. For myself, I regret that I was in
the thralls of trying to be. I had a sense of need and
a beguiling ability to satisfy those needs all during
the years that I drudged through school (your fourth
birthday was celebrated the day that I took part in
one of the Massachusetts Bar Examinations) while we
were living in Cambridge.*

*I don't know where it went wrong. I didn't know
what to expect of a child. I didn't know whether you
were usual or unusual for many months. In your
earliest weeks at home you cried with a persistence
and power that our English nanny thought was
extraordinary. But then look at your pictures—the
concentrated chubby little hand reaching out for the
candle on your first birthday cake. When you were
three, the nuns at St. Anne's just adored you and told
us you were an exceptional child—exceptional in needs
and in capacity to give, although you had problems
relating to people. You were good athletically and had
done well swimming. Of course, you and your horse
Peter Pan won a blue ribbon at Camp. The little girl
pictured on the dappled grey horse, the girl with her
cat. A really beautiful child with depths of feeling.*

And yet the problems were unignorable. The rather strange lady in the new progressive school gave me the bad news, which confirmed what I had been suspecting and halfway fearing, that you had a "behavior disorder"—problems of a severity that would require psychiatric help. Somehow there is a societal condemnation of failures of mental health, utterly at a variance with the problems of physical maladies. I remember reading of a mother's plaint saying that she wished her child had cancer rather than schizophrenia; maybe she meant that the pain was more finite in the case of cancer, and possibly she meant that at least people would understand and would try to help and would not condemn.

Almost nobody, irrespective of age, temperament or professional background, was able to cope or help us in any way with the realization, long in coming, that in some important way lessens the sense of personal failure for all.

We followed the advice of the professionals. Year followed year, and progress was not apparent. We were doing what "decent" people do in the hopes that the conventional wisdom would produce a "miracle." We went to consultants, had physical tests etc. There was, I felt, anger everywhere. I ultimately came to feel it as a personal threat, as a "war" for space in which I was obligated to engage or lose my existence. This sense of omnipresent anger is my strongest continuing recollection. I felt utterly helpless. Thus my child was angry beyond my capacity to affect. I never was able to find a means of communication that would give me access to this anger. I never felt the ability to say I love you, trust me, I want to help you. Instead, I was the enemy. What saddened me profoundly and saddens me still was that I was not the only enemy—

ultimately everybody became an enemy. I took you on special trips with me—one to New York City where we stayed at the Sherry Netherlands Hotel, once to Michigan where we looked at a performing arts camp that I prayed would let you do what you did so well, and finally to Switzerland, to school in a country I loved and where I went to school. I never was successful in communicating that I cared desperately for you, that I wanted to help.

Trying to live with anger is very difficult and painful. That we all survived in any physical or psychic state is a small miracle. I was always worried about Angus. The level of rage made it impossible for us to function as a family—we couldn't do anything as a family, eat meals, visit friends, play games or enjoy ourselves in our own house.

It began to seem to me that your anger towards me was threatening. Ultimately, I realized in the fall of 1970 that I couldn't spend any time in "peace" unless I had arranged for you to be somewhere else in the fall. That was when I concocted the notion of TASIS, a boarding school in Switzerland, and got you admitted somewhat late in the school year. We spent that Christmas in Africa at the Tsavo River Game Park; it was not a happy time. From there to your return in April to McLean was only a matter of three months. Your friends from school, Donna and Mimie were already there.

When you came back from Switzerland and asked to be admitted to McLean Hospital, I viewed it as a godsend. I literally had no idea what to do for you that was constructive and I had run out of ideas of ways in which I could put you in a position to help yourself.

Love, Your Dad

22

McLean Hospital

Despair banged on our front door, impatient, loud, and hard. Men's fists hit the wood; men's voices shouted something we couldn't hear; sirens wailed. Our son ran to the door, and five men, restless and uniformed, filled our front hall, two carrying axes. They tore apart our dinner.

"Where is it, where's the fire?" the leader demanded. I looked straight at him. I wanted to say, *Here it is, here, I am in danger of being extinguished. Put it out if you can, use your axes, if necessary.* I said nothing, but turned to look at Sandra. She hadn't moved, not a muscle. She was absolutely still and looking at her plate. There was no fire here.

I had gone to pick her up at the airport that afternoon. Returning from spring term at school in Switzerland, she looked so beautiful getting off the plane, just fifteen, in a brown leather skirt, boots, and a beige sweater. Her long, dark hair hung down her back. Her figure was slim, athletic, feminine, and striking. She looked at me with no expression. I thought perhaps the doctor had given her something. After a few pathetic attempts on my part to talk, we walked quietly to the car. Whatever I said felt hypocritical. Tomorrow we were admitting failure and taking her to a place I would be terrified to go to, even though she gave every indication of wanting to, or so the doctor in Switzerland had said.

Neither Bobby nor I knew anything firsthand about mental institutions. To me they were frightening and very dangerous places. The hospital Sandra was going to was a private one—supposedly one of the better ones in the country. I didn't know it then—people didn't talk about such things as mental illness in those days—but my great-grandmother Lucy Carnegie (mother's side), my aunt and uncle (father's side), and my stepfather had all been residents there.

I felt it was certain to be a godless place—a place of physical and mental pain, dark with violence and sudden terror, where someone out of control would approach your bed in the middle of the night. To leave our daughter in a place like that was the final crime, the definitive one. The endless imagined and real accusations that Bobby and I had been the cause of Sandra's illness rang in my mind.

Bobby and I were desperate and argued about what to do; sometimes our problems undermined all the support he gave me and left me feeling lonely and more desperate. Our lives were being eroded, our marriage threatened, and our son was paying a terrible price. We had to send him off at age ten to board at school during the week. It felt like a continued need for personal survival and that didn't leave much time or energy to function. For me, depression started around the edges. Anything that might separate me from Bobby overwhelmed me. Slowly and insidiously, Sandra was implanting the idea that Bobby should leave me. It was only later that I learned that "splitting"—experiencing others as either all good or all bad, idealizing or demonizing them—was part of the illness. At that time, while it was unconscious for me, Sandra touched a familiar nerve—she was like my mother, Lucy, another woman in the family who had pressed her strange version of reality on me. I was full of poison and unwanted.

Sandra packed a few things that night. The next morning was dreary and wet. The drive to the hospital took less than half an hour. No one talked. We were to have Sandra there by 9:30. I felt stunned and numb. When we arrived at the entrance, I was surprised by how attractive the grounds were— rolling hills, beautiful old oak trees, and large, attractive brick and wooden buildings. We found the admittance office and signed the correct papers. We had arranged for her to go to school there. An assistant came for Sandra and my daughter walked away without looking back. She was to be in the adolescent ward with her friend from school.

An image, a waking dream, kept running through my head that evening: a mother gave birth to a beautiful child, an exceptional child, a singing child who loved the sea and the outdoors, a child with a hint of real talent as an actress and an athlete, in many ways an interesting child, but a child who couldn't seem to take in love. Then one day the child looked up at the mother and said, "Look, Mother, I am bleeding, something is eating at my heart, help me." And it got worse, and the child screamed, "Save me, Mother, I am bleeding to death, save me, save me! Why don't you save me?" But the mother didn't know how to stop it, and she got covered with blood, and the child squirmed in agony and pain. She could neither die nor live, and was helpless, and the mother couldn't reach her child.

Sandra went to the hospital on Tuesday, April 26, 1971.

Having acknowledged a personal relationship to that dark side, the mourner may take a step that is socially more difficult by going public, coming out or speaking out as one who grieves.

At this point, mothers of handicapped children characteristically describe themselves as having entered a community (usually invisible to others) of people who are permanently changed by suffering, by grief. People, they say, are divided into two kinds: those who have known inescapable sorrow and those who have not. Inescapable or unassuming sorrow changes life itself. Because it cannot be changed, one's life-style and feelings must be changed to accommodate it. "Anyone who has been through such moments will know, and those who have not cannot know the vulnerability, the loss of innocence, the recognition of our inability to control our lives or to protect our children. I know what it is," Helen Featherstone writes, "to stand powerless before the gods, to see a child I love hurt by forces I can neither name nor control."[1]

---

[1] Barbara H. Davis, Director of Women's Studies, University of Oklahoma, 1985.

23

Sandra Has Been Loved

I was grateful that my hand didn't shake as I reached up to push the bell at the entrance to the maximum-security ward. Sandra had been in the adolescent ward at first, but after eight months things fell apart and the staff there couldn't control her, so she was moved to the locked ward. Her diagnosis was schizophrenia.

Standing there in front of that enormous eighteenth-century brick building with its heavy, oval wooden door, I felt like a child summoned to the principal's office so the appropriate punishment could be meted out. I put my hand down to smooth my skirt and noticed a spot on the front of it. I tried to pull my black cashmere sweater over it but it wouldn't reach. Suddenly everything about me felt like it was about to pull apart. My sweater was too tight; I gave it a violent tug to stretch it, praying no one saw me. My hair blew over my mouth. My breath was so shallow that l felt as if I might suffocate on the spot.

I pushed the buzzer and the door clicked to let me in. Before me stood a very thin young man. I came to call him Cerberus—the gatekeeper of the underworld—because he was always there when I rang. I was afraid to look in his eyes, eyes that let me know there was no compass that could keep the unspeakable from happening, and in any event it would mean nothing to him. No pain, no remorse, no pleasure in his kingdom of the dead.

"Yeah?"

His face was terribly pale and covered with gouged and bleeding pimples clustered around his nose.

"Yeah?"

"I have come to see Sandra." I pulled back. I hadn't expected this raw, chilling energy. Where were the nurses?

"Yeah, she's here. You her mother?"

A stern voice came from somewhere inside: "Richard, you are not allowed to open that door, please get back here."

"You motherfuck . . . shit you . . ."

A young woman appeared from around the corner and before greeting me she addressed Richard again.

"Come now, Richard, let's go back."

Richard stood there evidently undecided for a moment, and I smiled to myself at the relief I felt, having the tension broken by this Richard—at least he looked more disorganized than I.

Richard leaned forward and threw both arms straight up in the air in a languid, helpless sort of way, then reached for his face and, without looking at either of us, departed toward the ward, but not without a loud, hard, final word on the subject. "Pick it and eat it, pick it and eat it, pick it and eat it!" he shouted down the hall.

"You must be Sandra's mother. My name is Elly. I'm a nurse here. Come in, we've been expecting you."

I nodded and stepped over the threshold. The last two months had been such a nightmare that sometimes my own sense of the most familiar things shimmered and weakened and the ground seemed to rock slowly. The last time I had been permitted to see Sandra, it had been in a less forbidding building, not in the locked ward under maximum security. They hadn't been able to cope with her anger and her threatening to cut her wrists—a new development—in the more open adolescent ward.

I walked toward Sandra's room, past the airless, dreary living room in which there was always a TV on, nearly drowned out by the crying and shouting of the most acutely ill adolescents. After knocking and getting no response, I slowly pushed her door open. Sandra was sitting on her bed propped up against the wall—sagging against it, her head hung over.

"Sandra." No response. "Sandra, may I come in?" She raised her head and slowly turned toward me. "What is the matter, Sandra? What's happening?" She shook her head ever so slightly, saliva sliding down the left side of her face, her mouth pulled open and down to the left. Her eyes couldn't focus and her hands shook. She was either unwilling or unable to wipe away the drool. I moved toward the bed. I wanted to touch her. As I got closer, I sensed she didn't want that. I stood there wondering if I should sit on her bed and hold her, but I was afraid of her reaction. I closed my eyes and slowly left the room, making my way to the nurses' station. I rapped on the thick glass.

"What on earth has happened to Sandra?"

"She got badly out of hand, extremely angry—it took three men to hold her down, and we put her on heavy doses of Thorazine."

"Is that safe? She looks terrible! Can she breathe? Shouldn't someone be with her? Isn't there some other way?"

"She'll be fine, it will wear off."

I felt an edge of bitterness, coupled with the insight that here in the hospital they couldn't handle her either. Certainly drugging her beyond her capacity to control herself was no answer. Once again, I was tormented by the suspicion that Bobby and I were partly to blame for letting this happen. I found myself looking at the nurse and thinking, *Yes, Sandra comes from a family with tremendous energy. She's also brilliant and hurting and beyond control. I should know. It has been going on in our home for some years now. I kept trying to tell the doctors that I didn't have any tranquilizers and didn't know how to help.*

The most wearing thing of all was Sandra's relentless accusation that we didn't love her—or rather, I didn't love her. I—not Bobby—was the one expected to bear the guilt, to feel always that I hadn't done enough, that I was the cause of all her pain. The thought, once implanted, never left me—and never has to this day. Only how? How had I done it? And what was it I had done?

Now, standing in the maximum-security ward for adolescents, I stared down at a hideous pea-green carpet filled with so many burnt cigarette holes that it almost looked like a floral design. The dreary green walls were bare except for marks and scratches. The green vinyl furniture had chunks taken out of it so that the dirty yellow foam protruded like pus. The nurses' station, a thick glass prism with a large lock, stood out like a shining diamond against the drab greenness.

"Jesus, couldn't they make this place a bit more cheerful?" I said out loud, mostly to myself.

Elly overheard me and replied, "It's too bad, but it's very difficult to keep things up in this ward." She asked me to wait in the room off the nurses' station while she got a key to let me out. I wished that Bobby were with me. I remembered my last conversation with Sandra. She had called begging to come home: "Please, please, I want to come home and get out of here." I answered lamely, "I don't think the hospital would let you right now; soon I'm sure." I had hung up and felt sick.

In the locked ward, I leaned against the wall. A heavyset girl with black hair sat in one of the chairs chain-smoking, while down the hall a thin, lovely girl was walking back and forth with a nurse and crying. Every so often she would start to collapse and cry out to the nurse, "Get them off me, get them off, they are crawling all over me," as she frantically brushed her hands over her body.

Two weeks later, when I returned, Richard was still

hanging around the front door, only this time his right hand was heavily bandaged and he wasn't voicing his usual prayer. I asked Elly what had happened. "I'm afraid he cut off three of his fingers," Elly replied. She turned away, ending the conversation.

My mind rocketed around in panic. My thoughts these days kept startling me—they were often vulgar, or bitter and shocking. Now I could hear my mind shouting at me:

Oh God, now he can't pick it and eat it anymore. That's why he is silent. I desperately wanted to get away. *The crazy must get crazier in here. Chaos, man turned against himself, and our daughter is here. They don't know the diagnosis, so what's the treatment?*

I looked at Elly and asked, "How can you stand it?"

"There's a big turnover of staff in this ward," she replied.

Three months later, after Sandra was out of solitary confinement, we all went back into family therapy, which was useless. Sandra refused to talk to us or to her psychiatrist, who wouldn't talk either and just glared at Bobby. I disliked him instantly. How could we change things or help Sandra if no one would talk?

About two months later, I was called and asked to see Dr. Campbell. I had been surprised to see how much better Sandra seemed. Dr. Campbell, a Scotsman whose accent I found hard to understand, came right to the point.

"I must inform you that Sandra was planning to run off with a man who was a member of our staff here in the hospital."

"She is only sixteen." I could hardly breathe, and felt a surge of anger and frustration. "How old is he?"

"He's twenty-eight and has a wife and a child. We've just discovered that he and Sandra had been having an affair for quite some time."

"She's sick! How could you let that happen?" I shouted at him. I stared at him and shook my head. "The staff are supposed to protect her."

Dr. Campbell, who would turn out to be one of the few professionals at McLean I could relate to, said in his soft voice and thick Scots accent: "Well, it's not so bad you know, because she feels she has been loved."

I thought, *Your implication is that she has not been loved. It is all right to send our daughter here at great expense and have your incompetent staff take advantage of her! Is this what you recommend for treatment after criticizing us for our lack of control and not caring about her? You can't control her anger and rage, you just drug her out of her mind and allow your staff to sexually abuse her in the name of love.* But I didn't say any of those things. I wish I had, but I was too stunned.

"Loved?" I whispered aloud. "Loved?" *But her family loves her. I love her, her father loves her; we all do.*

This was when I began subtly to wonder if it was the child's illness, which they couldn't heal, that was destroying our family and causing me, as a mother, to cease to function in a well and happy life. Maybe it wasn't Sandra's fault, but it wasn't ours either. The psychiatrists were hurting our family.

Later that week, the nurse on duty called the house. I answered the phone with a feeling of deep unease.

"We are calling to inform you that Sandra has had a grave setback, and we have had to heavily sedate her again and put her in solitary confinement."

"What happened?"

"Do you remember her friend on the ward, Alice?"

"Yes, we know the family as well."

"I'm sorry to say, Alice went home for the weekend, had a bad argument with her family, and on her way back to the hospital she jumped off the Mystic River Bridge."

I closed my eyes and slowly sat down on the edge of the chair.

"Oh, God help me, just help me, now, now . . ." and then I heard a small ringing voice in my head: *Sandra has not cut her fingers off . . . Sandra has not jumped off the bridge . . . Sandra has been loved . . .*

24

Tempting Death

Over the next few years, Sandra was allowed to come home from McLean Hospital for the weekends occasionally when she was well enough. One Friday night in the summer at Crescent Farm, when Sandra was eighteen, everyone had tiptoed around trying not to set her off, but Saturday started poorly. Sandra wanted to use the car, but she didn't have a license. She could still drive on the farm, but we didn't know what kind of drugs she was on, legitimate or otherwise. All the patients on her ward managed to procure drugs one way or another. She had run away from the hospital four months ago only to return eight days later, drugged and ill. We refused to let her take the car.

You didn't say *no* to Sandra. She wreaked havoc, screaming, "You have always tried to kill me!"—an accusation that rang through my mind, the very words I had heard my mother speak to my sister, not to me. Now, what I had always managed to avoid was directed at me. "You're ruining my life so you two can survive!" she shouted, and stormed out the back door. The weekend was shattered, but we let her go, feeling she was safe enough on the farm. Besides, we had the keys to the car.

About half an hour later, my niece came running into the house, all out of breath.

"She's running away—I'm not supposed to tell."

"Sandra? Where is she?"

"A man she's been involved with is meeting her down by Route 77."

"How did she get there?"

"She took the three-wheeler."

Bobby, normally a cautious driver, drove very fast. We caught up with them just as Sandra was reaching the designated meeting place. The man had a large Harley-Davidson and wore a black jacket. Bobby threw the three-wheeler into the truck, and Sandra after it. There was a huge fight. I was screaming at Sandra, "How could you do this?" over and over, and Bobby was furious, not speaking, just acting. We drove Sandra back to the hospital immediately and held our breath crossing the Mystic River Bridge, where her friend had jumped off a month ago. She was put in solitary confinement, where she was to stay off and on for roughly two months.

I went to visit Sandra when I finally got permission. My usual gatekeeper had been sent to a state hospital, probably for life, minus the three fingers he had managed to cut off. Elly unlocked the doors and we walked down a long corridor. Sandra had been in solitary confinement for three weeks. At the end of the hall, there were four rooms with thick glass windows set in metal doors. Elly walked up to one of the doors, all the time speaking in a measured litany. "We open the door every hour . . . check on the patients every fifteen minutes . . . they do get out to walk, it's the law . . ."

I didn't hear any more after that. The door opened and Sandra was in there, sitting on a thin mattress on the cement floor. The room was very small and there was nothing in it. A small window with bars let in some light. The walls were a dull green. Sandra looked up, and I squatted down to be at her eye level. It was the first time in weeks that she had agreed to see me. I struggled to reach for someplace inside me where I could understand what my child was feeling, what she was going through . . . but there was nothing. I had never experienced the kind of personal hell she was going through. There was only an ache in my heart for her.

Sandra was still drugged but not so heavily. Both of her wrists had gauze bandages, even though she had been under twenty-four-hour personal surveillance. She sat there without saying a word. Scratched on the bare wall above her head was a sentence: "I am me and I have the right to be."

"Sandra, did you write that?"

She just nodded in response and handed me a crumpled piece of paper she held in her fist: a poem she had written. In the poem she said, "Why have they locked me up for being angry? I have a hidden razor." She had cut her wrists.

I couldn't speak.

Sandra finally left McLean at the age of twenty-one. She seemed better, we were never clear why. She moved to a halfway house and then came to Crescent Farm to live.

She was writing a book, and Bobby and I were trying to help her get it published. It was a brilliant, candid exploration of her pain. Sandra and I never discussed it; perhaps it was too painful for both of us. I tried years later, but the right moment never came. In her book she wrote: "If someone could love me unconditionally—parents can give unconditional love—the battle with rage would take me over and would fly like bullets and bombs at people."

The rage must be tremendous. What could be crueler than to live on this earth and not be able to feel loved or to love oneself? I think, at the end of the day, we must truly love ourselves, and only then can we love others. Sandra was loved but couldn't feel it. I wasn't loved but had to learn to accept love.

Sandra wrote the following when she was about eighteen:

I was driven to absolute fury. The power struggles always became rapidly clear running back into my being a waterfall of intense, subtle vicious survival

> *all there—like they never left, and I'd be fighting for*
> *control, control, control. It seems to be the essence of*
> *human nature and being in such a vulnerable posi-*
> *tion stripped away of any acts one could have and left*
> *one fighting like an animal for dignity, one's rights,*
> *and control.*
>
> *Although I wished I had been more integrated*
> *with myself and the world and been able to let myself*
> *react and express myself more appropriately and ef-*
> *fectively, I was glad that I did allow myself to blow in*
> *some form, for it felt like holding onto all that "stuff"*
> *would have created some kind of organic sickness in*
> *me, be it psychological or emotional, such as psychosis,*
> *etc., or be it physical, such as cancer or heart disease,*
> *etc.*

I think Sandra did have some unusual insight into her condition from time to time, but the rage and anger overtook her just as terrible physical pain would. It was devastating to her to have no control.

25

Psychiatrists and Witches

Over the years I had gone to four different psychiatrists to find some help for both my daughter and myself, beginning with the disastrous experience at the Jackson Clinic when she was six. While Sandra was at McLean, I had three different psychiatrists: Dr. Edward Daniels; a very stiff Cambridge intellectual lady (we didn't fit too well) who died three months after I started with her; and finally (I was getting a bit fed up with the profession by this time) a reasonable-looking doctor who was Jewish and Irish. I thought this was a good combination, but after three visits during which he resolutely refused to speak (standard practice among strict Freudian analysts of that day), I got up and announced, "I think you're crazier than I am." He burst out laughing, but I was out the door.

Dr. Daniels, who answered the phone, opened his mail, and discussed patients with other therapists during my visits, was an eminent Boston psychiatrist on the top rung at McLean. He worked out of his office in a secluded and expensive suburb of Boston. The hospital staff picked him to work through problems between Sandra and me. He told me I should be in analysis, but Dr. Daniels was insistent, and had me lie down on the couch while he sat behind me out of view.

After about a year of this, I began to feel I was being taken advantage of. I also felt something else was wrong, aside from the fact that I was paying him to open his mail and talk on the phone when I badly needed help and wasn't getting it; I kept feeling an odd aversion to him, so I left. We never really talked about Mother or my problem with Sandra. It was hard to talk to someone who was on the phone talking with other psychiatrists about patients. Some years after I left him, he appeared on the front page of the *Boston Globe*—he'd slept with at least three of his patients. I was stunned. This was a doctor whom I needed to trust in order to deal with the terrible pain and depression I was beginning to feel—and all the while he was having affairs with his patients! If he had tried anything on me, I would have lost my timidity and flattened him.

Dr. Daniels was heavy, short, and bald. Nothing about him was attractive. To my mind he was a clever, sarcastic bully. What was his power? How did this sick man seduce who knows how many women and what terrible damage did he do during his expensive fifty-minute orgies? To my mind he was another scatterer of seeds among the ladies— just like my father.

Accused Doctor Suspended[2]
Boston Globe (BG)—Thursday April 26, 1990
By Alison Bass, Globe Staff

An influential Chestnut Hill psychiatrist has been suspended from the staff of McLean Hospital, and expelled from the Boston Psychoanalytical Society and Institute after an investigation by the society into charges that he had sexually abused female patients.

Edward M. Daniels, 69, was also placed on a leave of absence by Harvard Medical School pending an investigation by the state Board of Regis-

---

[2] Third edition, Metro section, page 41. Copyright © 1990, Globe Newspaper Company, Republished with permission.

tration in Medicine. He denies the allegations of abuse.

The actions reflect a major change in recent months in the institutional response to complaints about sexual misconduct by health professionals, officials and observers said.

It is the first time that McLean, a prestigious psychiatric hospital in Belmont, has suspended a staff psychiatrist suspected of sexually abusing patients, a spokeswoman said. It is only the second time the Psychoanalytic Society has ousted a member suspected of such behavior.

Psychiatrists said Daniels was perhaps the best-known training analyst in the Boston area, where he has practiced for more than 40 years.

Dr. Elizabeth Reid, president of the Psychoanalytic Society, said it expelled Daniels after a "long and very careful" investigation.

"I give these groups a lot of credit for what they did," commented Jan Wohlberg, an advocate for women who have been abused by therapists, who was herself abused in this way. Wohlberg said she has witnessed a sea change in the way such cases are handled.

"Seven years ago, these institutions knew what happened with these women and Daniels and they didn't do anything, so it certainly looks like change is happening," she said. "Organizations are recognizing that they have to police themselves, but it's also sad, because people who are prominent role models are turning out to have feet of clay."

Reid said the Psychoanalytic Society based its decision on complaints against Daniels by two women, who had also recently filed malpractice suits against him. In their suits, both women allege that Daniels subjected them to "years of sexual abuse" while treating them in the 1960s.

A third patient sued Daniels in 1982, alleging that he had had sexual relations with her over a six-year period while treating her for depression. That suit, filed in US District Court, was settled out of court.

During Sandra's last year in McLean we had a call from one of the doctors there; I'll call him Dr. Shul. He asked us to come see him. Bobby and I were curious about the meeting and arrived with some trepidation.

Dr. Shul got straight to the point: "We have diagnosed Sandra as having a borderline personality disorder, a fairly new diagnosis in the field."

Bobby and I looked at each other. "Well, is this just one more diagnosis?" Bobby asked. Dr. Shul ignored him.

"Borderline personality disorder is an illness that can be severe, chronic, and persistent. The suicide rate is high. Borderlines are unable to regulate their impulses, and there's a great deal of uncontrolled rage. Some in the profession no longer believe that a dysfunctional family is the only cause." He also said that most psychiatrists are reluctant to work with borderlines and most therapies really don't seem to help.

At this point I interrupted. Did Dr. Shul mean to suggest that the borderline's reality is so powerful it can rob parents and others of theirs? One of the saddest consequences of mental illness is the way it can tear apart a family, and often a marriage—everyone feels so vulnerable and to blame.

But if the doctors can't cope and don't want to deal with these children, how is the family to survive? How is a marriage to survive? Does this new diagnosis still blame the mother, as with schizophrenia ("schizophrenogenic mothers" was a commonly employed term), and encourage the patient to blame her as well? For years the psychiatric profession demonized mothers—like the witches of Salem, they were accused of causing the children to be crazy and then hanged for it. At this point my anger and sense of injustice were probably healthy for me. I could still feel the rope burning around my neck.

"There is a high incidence of wrist slashing, promiscuity, and impulsive behavior," Dr. Shul continued. "If drinking or drugs become involved, it can become a serious obstacle to healing."

He told us about the work of Dr. Otto Kernberg, who some years later would confirm her diagnosis as a border-line personality—a condition characterized by volatile and histrionic behavior; inability to maintain a stable sense of self; difficulty in relationships; and worst of all, paranoia and suicidal behavior. (It never occurred to the doctors at McLean in the 1970s that the illness might run in the family—from my mother to her granddaughter; Mother was hardly ever mentioned.)

"It's a new diagnosis," Dr. Shul said, "and I'm afraid patients often do not react to therapy. Therapists don't like to work with them and there are now no drugs that work as well as we would like, although a regulated combina-tion can sometimes help. They refuse to take responsibility for themselves. It's always someone else's fault and their boundaries are very weak. The families to date have taken a lot of blame they don't deserve, although environment can have some effect."

"That sounds familiar," said Bobby. "We've been accused of everything you can imagine. It doesn't mat-ter what we do, the result is always the same, blaming her parents, never herself. Another self-damaging act or suicide attempt, another rage-filled event, another failed relationship." Bobby paused. "Another attempt to split her mother and me up."

Dr. Shul just nodded.

Bobby and I were stunned and relieved that at last we heard a diagnosis that seemed to fit, but at the same time it was devastating. Bobby, almost in a whisper, said, "It's a life sentence for all of us."

The doctor didn't reply. Instead he handed us a brochure from a mental health association and said, "This might help. I'm sorry."

It was shortly after this visit in 1978 that Sandra moved to live in a little family house on Crescent Island. As far as we knew, there was no hope of recovery from borderline personality and no medicine that helped.

That was when I discovered I had cancer.

26

Cancer

I have left undone those things which I ought to have done, and I have done those things which I ought not to have done, and there is no health in me . . .

That phrase, adapted from the Book of Common Prayer, kept going through my head as I lay in the hospital after the operation, slowly waking and hearing the doctor say to Bobby that I had a fifty-fifty chance of survival. The cancer had metastasized to lymph nodes in my right breast. They had performed a mastectomy to remove as much of it as they could. I lay there trying to grasp the concept that I might die.

In the ancient epic of the Mahabharata, it says the greatest miracle of all is that man is going to die and he doesn't even know it. I remember Bobby leaping out of the chair toward the doctor as he said: "She has a fifty-fifty chance of survival if she tries a new treatment."

It wasn't until the second day in the hospital that I began to understand there was a chance I might live by having a new chemotherapy treatment. In those two days, I believe I was further away from dying than I was when I was fully alive in the world because life appeared precious. My constant thoughts were of what I had left undone—I could not leave the children. Angus would be fine; he had his father. But I could not leave Sandra. No matter how little help I was to her, I could not leave her now.

Sandra and I had a long talk right after I got out of the hospital. She said, "If you're going to die, we better talk."

"I think I'll be all right, darling."

We talked for three hours. We spent some of the time on familiar themes, the primary one being that I should leave her father (an instance of what we now knew to call splitting); but the other persistent themes typical of borderlines, the rage directed at us for being the cause of all her pain and the anger at not feeling loved, were less in evidence that evening. We mainly talked about her future. She wanted her own house on Crescent Island. She wanted to get a horse and keep it in the barn with the other horses. I began to think the possibility that I might die bothered Sandra. I was so exhausted that the tears started, and Sandra came across the room and gave me a hug.

All during my illness, Sandra was thoughtful and kind; once she gave me a beautiful crystal bowl that, when tapped, gave off a clear and healing sound. She also gave me a necklace, a gold triangle made of opal—my birthstone. On the back, she had engraved, "We live for those we love." She had changed the Sherlock Crest, which was Irish and belonged to Lucy's family, from "We die for those we love."

Sandra and I explored all sorts of alternative medicine for her and me. We went to psychics and astrologers, read tarot cards, and explored other healing possibilities. It was a good time between us. When I started to improve, Bobby and I explored many things together too, such as acupuncture and nutrition. We didn't understand the effects of stress in those days. We became vegetarians for seven years. We tried psychics, shamanic healing, eventually Jungian therapy and meditation. Perhaps Bobby's care was the most healing of all.

27

Reprieve

Silence vibrating is creation
Silence flowing is love
Silence omitted is suffering
Silence allowed is rest
Silence received is joy
—Maharishi

Bobby's father died when I was halfway through my chemotherapy, which was to last for two years every three weeks. I remember going to the funeral feeling a bit fragile. I had always been fond of my father-in-law; we shared an interest in the workings of God. I don't remember what part of the funeral it was, but suddenly, when thinking about him, I was overcome with immense joy. It just poured through me and I felt that all was well with him, that maybe he was even happier now than he had ever been. I have had that experience once or twice since.

While trying to keep up my strength, I began thinking that I needed to do something else to heal—other than what the doctors prescribed. I felt it wasn't only the body but also the spirit that needed healing now. Instinctively I felt I needed a good deal of quiet time and silence, a real rest from the distress caused by my father, and Sandra, now twenty-two, and even the dance company, which was stressful at times.

I had no idea where to begin. In those days, the nutrition department at the Massachusetts General Hospital was no help, so I started taking courses at healing places like Interface outside Boston; going to a cancer counselor who introduced me to the works of Carl Jung; and getting my mantra at the

Transcendental Meditation Center in Cambridge. You name it, I tried it. We even went to Esalen, the notorious retreat that helped create the "human potential movement." The sexual revolution for which it was famous passed us by. My sister, who came with us, wore a swimsuit in the hot tub.

I tried acupuncture, but I couldn't tell what the results were. Chinese breathing taught by a "master" was incredibly helpful. I was feeling a good deal of pain in my arms. A group of about eight of us lay on the floor, and after learning backwards breathing for five days, we all started screaming, as if we were giving birth. My arms and shoulders were in pain, I'm guessing now, from stress and breathing in a fight-or-flight mode—short, shallow breaths that deprive the muscles and nerves of oxygen and make them tighten up. The deep Chinese breathing released the muscles. When I walked out of there, the pain was gone.

The most fascinating healer was a woman who had trained and worked as an engineer, and then one day discovered that she could heal people, but soon she had to stop healing because it became overwhelming, but continued to lecture. I was taking a two-year course on polarity massage, which teaches how to move energy in and through the body. There were about forty of us at the course. She wandered through the group as we were working with each other and ended up by me. She put her hands high on my back on the side where I'd had the mastectomy. "This is where the problem is." She leaned over and whispered, "I feel you have the ability to heal others." I nodded and suddenly felt as if I had touched an electrical fence. I was the only person she healed. I feel that her touch is one of the reasons I am still here.

There was one other wonderful healing lesson I was to have. Bobby and I went for a week in Virginia to learn about shamanic healing. Michael Harner, well known in the shamanic world, was teaching. It was to be a very special week for me as I received my "power animal." There were about thirty of us in the group, and we soon were given the task of going down into the earth to receive our power animal, to "visualize" the place where you would find him or her. I remember being amazed when three people who didn't know each other went to a place that they could explain in detail to each other.

I found myself by a river and there was the mourning dove, the bird that made the sound I loved so much as a child – I was delighted. All my life birds have played a part; from the white dove coming into the kitchen when our brother-in-law died, the birds that came three times when my mother died, and the one that woke me up to let me know I had cancer and to go back to the hospital and confront the doctor. They fit comfortably with my north wind, and in churches' stained glass windows they are depicted as bringing the spirit down to the earth and taking the spirits of the dead upward. All my life, the morning dove has sung for me her haunting melancholy song. Now she is my "power animal" and her song and presence an enormous comfort. So many connections in my life I am grateful for.

But the most lasting and fascinating journey to the unconscious—aside from Jungian analysis, which I started at this time, and am still involved with today, some thirty years later—were the ideas and practices that I found in the Transcendental Meditation movement started by Maharishi Mahesh Yogi. The little I had read about the Vedic philosophy captured my imagination, and when I read that the Maharishi said it was "all right to be happy," I was hooked. For those who came from a Protestant background, happiness was not allowed.

After I got my mantra, I went to a three-week Transcendental Meditation course in the Catskills to learn the flying and levitating sutras. We were called *siddhas*—practitioners who have achieved a higher level of consciousness. There was a man named Deepak Chopra—destined to become a world-renowned spiritual guide—whom we teased because in the beginning he was having a lot of trouble flying, as they called it, though it felt more like hopping.

We got together with Deepak and his wife, Rita, quite often; once they visited us in Maine. Years later, in the 1980s, when we were living in England (Bobby spent a lot of time there on various business ventures), Deepak called and asked if we would like to go to the Maharishi's birthday; he had become the Maharishi's right-hand man. We flew to Vlödrop, Holland, where the Maharishi lived. There must have been three hundred people in the hall. The birthday celebration lasted three days. Throughout that whole time the Maharishi spoke nonstop and never left the stage from early morning until evening. I only saw him take a little something to drink.

Our appointment was at 3:00 A.M. on the third day. We arrived to find the Maharishi wide awake and with a slim gentleman all in white cloth very solemnly sitting next to him. Bobby and the Maharishi began to talk. I don't remember the conversation exactly, only that Bobby is a Sagittarius and very outspoken and not quite as much in awe as I was of the Maharishi. The next thing we knew the slender man in white began to giggle, and then laugh, and all of a sudden, he was on the floor rolling with laughter. We found out later that he had been told we were a very stuffy, uptight old Boston couple, and he found the conversation between Bobby and the Maharishi hilarious, as most people have enormous reverence for the Maharishi, and Bobby, my Sagittarius, acted and spoke as if Maharishi were just an ordinary person.

At the very end, I got to ask the Maharishi a question. I asked, "Is meditating a small death?" Maharishi answered yes. I didn't have a chance to ask all the questions Maharishi's answer brought up in my mind, but it was enough to sustain me and give clues to my other thoughts. I began to feel that "death was the teacher," the title of a chapter ("The Katha"), from *The Upanishads* (very ancient Hindu wisdom). I added, death is the Teacher of the spirit. I learned later that the small death is really called the Gap in which there is the process of transcending and in which the Light of God is experienced. This is one reason why meditators who consistently experience the 'small death,' the Gap and are not so bothered by the prospect of corporeal death. I believe, I understand, "The whole purpose of this cosmic game is to live that 'Death' experience while living and to establish the Light of God 24/7."[2]

What's more, we heard later that Maharishi said Bobby was a good man who could make a huge difference – a grand compliment – and he said that I was very intelligent. How I treasured that comment. He also called Bobby at home in Maine quite a few times after that, but Bobby wasn't quite aware of the tremendous compliment. I often wondered what we missed.

I am convinced Maharishi knew anything he wanted to and maybe was only barely here physically towards the end of his life. When he was dying many years later in 2008, he called all of the Sidhas together and taught us how to be happy. What a gift to leave us with. During the years, we made very dear friends in the movement and have come in contact with one or two of the gentlemen who were his right hand in the world.

Our visit and opportunity to meet the Maharishi is one of the highlights of my life – it gave me hints of the value of silence, and a glimpse of tremendous knowledge and a life that can be open to all possibility. Bliss is the name for those who meditate for years, which is how the Dalai Lama describes it too in his own way. The Maharishi has brought us back that knowledge if we choose to pursue it. I feel like I carry a visual image of him in my heart.

[2] Vedic knowledge

*

Bobby and I went to Northern Island that fall after my chemotherapy was over; I felt well enough, but I needed some time to rest and think quietly. In the stillness and warmth of the first day of autumn, I lay rocking gently in a hammock overlooking the bay. In the days that followed, my thoughts kept drifting downstream like endless bubbles on the surface of a deep river, spiraling gently up to the top to settle on the surface and slip into the past.

I often rose before sunrise because I considered that time of day, like the sunset, to be sacred. The awakening of the soul in the soft early morning light—what is this gift of grace in the soft light? What is this longing? Is it to return without fear from where we came? I listened to that endless voice inside my head, which said, *Listen, listen, be patient, be quiet, and you will hear what you need to know.*

Something ran through my body at that moment, through my blood and bones, and something connected, so much joy and longing, and I was grateful that I hadn't died.

The dragonfly painted on my coffee mug spread its wings, the tomatoes in the garden burst to a shining red, and the large birch tree moved slowly, whispering, *Remember, remember.* The first morning light acted like a scrim, masking the scene behind it in another dimension, making the scene shift and change.

There was no sound. The light had a crystal quality, a shimmering, and every indication from nature was to be silent, so I watched and waited and wondered in all the stillness, rocking gently in the hammock. Rocking again in the ribs of the large boat, the breeze gently caressed my cheek and tears streamed down my face. I was neither sad nor happy, but at peace.

Then the light shifted, barely perceptibly, and the scrim slid away from the sea, the tall pines, the rocks, and the island itself, and they all looked ordinary again. As if by some mysterious signal, the birds started clamoring in the big tree by the house and the air was filled with the sound of singing. Seagulls chattered and the loons cried out to each other. With this announcement, the day began. I could feel my soul retreating, my breath losing its quiet rhythm of the heart, and felt the anxious dance of relationships, the return of lists, of fixing this and doing that, of the general pattern of life beginning.

But even now I still very faintly hear that voice encouraging me, *Remember, remember*, until the world intrudes on my peace, my silence, and the morning light fades from my mind.

28

Crescent Island Life with Father

One day in 1975 my father was standing absolutely still at the end of the quay looking into the storm, his long gray cloak whipping around his body while white spray flew past him. Behind him his large house of gray stone and wooden beams was being battered by waves that were hitting the roof and tapping at the large picture windows. The quay was slowly falling into the sea.

Our caretaker, Phil McPhee, had been walking down the beach. When he told me what he had seen, I smiled to myself. I guessed that the storm and the destruction it wrought had quieted my father's restless, angry spirit. While he lived, he dominated everyone who shared Crescent Island with him. Some of us on the farm would wish for constant hurricanes so that his stormy, destructive spirit wouldn't be turned against his children or turn us against each other. But my father cared deeply for Crescent Island. Every morning in the summer he would swim before breakfast in the cold Atlantic water with whomever he could convince to go with him. Then he would head down to the stables, stopping at the dairy to meet and chat with the farm manager before riding through the woods and down the beaches, stopping on a hill overlooking the Periwinkle River. I remember, as a child, joining him once to see the river flow out to the sea.

After Lucy divorced him, he remarried and had three children, a boy and two girls, and acquired two stepchildren; he then married a third time and acquired three stepdaughters. Around the time of his marriage to his second wife, he started building what some in the family called his "chicken coops," into which he placed single ladies and attractive, willing wives. There were those who claimed they could hear him flapping and crowing every morning before he started his rounds.

One evening when he had been drinking, he walked over and stood right in front of me and started shouting, "Your Grandfather Carnegie was a no-good bum!" He kept at it. Having been very fond of my grandfather, I answered, "I cared about Grampa Negie! He was not a bum!" The next thing I knew he'd thrown his glass of liquor in my face. I took one step forward but refrained from clobbering him. Most people were afraid of him; I never was. It was a long time before I would see him again. My father had become a stranger.

I began to realize in later years that my father had taught me about anger—sometimes murderous anger. He had taught me about my shadow, that side of ourselves that we'd rather not know about. He had the uncanny ability of knowing how to hurt his children and in some cases turn them against each other. I began to feel fortunate that he had not been part of my childhood.

There was one incident with him that changed my views about life and about myself. After we moved to Crescent Island, we had two dirt roads, about two miles long, going out from our house to the main road. One of the roads, on which we had the right of way, was in good condition; the other was barely passable, and often impassable in bad weather. The next thing we knew, Father had hired a huge crane to drag a twenty-foot-long steel beam across our road and dug a large ditch in front of it. Not only was it dangerous for us to use the other road, but we didn't have the funds to fix it—the cost would have been considerable—and we had old people on our part of the farm who were ill. No fire truck or ambulance could have made it through on the nearly unusable road, and it was the only inside road through the forest to the beaches.

We had to consider a lawsuit. We had a mud hole in front of our house that was supposed to be a small pond; my father had built it for one of his lady friends. It was an eyesore, so we decided to pump some water out of a large nearby pond to fill it up. Father decided one afternoon to destroy the pipe. So he got his handyman, Mr. Benson, to get an axe and drove over and proceeded to chop the pipe to pieces. I heard poor Mr. Benson got ill, he was so nervous.

This last act coursed through my nervous system like a series of electric wires. Between Sandra's years at McLean and worrying about her on Crescent Island and my father, I was coming unstrung.

It was mud season on the farm. One night it was pouring, which made the road worse, when my sister-in-law's nanny, who still lived with her, fainted. They put her in a car and headed out the road only to get stuck. They finally managed to get out, but I was irate. What if Nanny had been seriously ill?

The next day, a wet, foggy day, I got in my car without my raincoat and managed to drive to the barrier, having no idea what I intended to do but feeling capable of violence. I wanted my father to stop destroying and hurting his children and getting away with it—to stop driving people off the farm and endangering people's lives. I decided, perhaps naïvely, as I crawled over the wet, cold steel barrier, that I would do whatever it took to stop him—a dangerous thought in my state of mind; I had no idea how dangerous.

I noticed an old broken-down wooden horse next to the barrier. I went up to it and tore off some of the boards and started dragging them up to his house, which was about thirty yards away, and then up the steps. I stood panting at the large wooden door. I pushed the door open and stood in the hall on the redbrick floor, which I had always hated—I thought the color was evil and cold. I stood there holding my weapon and shouted, "Father, Father!"

He suddenly appeared out of the dining room, saw it was I, and opened his arms wide. "Millicent, Millicent! What a wonderful surprise," he said.

I heaved the old piece of wood at him, which fell short, then leapt at him, yelling, "Move the barrier!" He warded off my blows but I realized that he was old and unable to protect himself. I backed away, confused, and ran out the door. I left with the clear understanding that I could have hurt my father—the desire had been there. I remembered how Goethe had said he couldn't imagine any crime he wasn't capable of committing. Yet when the moment came, I couldn't—I never could have hurt him.

I cannot judge my father any more than I can judge myself. I think if he had been able, he would have cared for all of us. It really didn't occur to me until much later that he was probably not able to. Early on, I had to believe he was healthy, for I couldn't accept that he was ill too. But over time, I have come to believe he was not well. He was incapable of coping with his anger and his impulse to hurt others. It was clear that he couldn't run a business. It's a widely held belief that if someone is wealthy and doesn't work it's because they don't have to, but I believe a healthy person enjoys working, and that mental illness strikes indiscriminately, regardless of wealth, and kills the ability to work in those it afflicts. My father's promiscuity and his inability to keep up his farm or have deep relationships with people concealed a huge energy and intelligence. He also had a real talent for insight, as does Sandra, and an uncanny sense of what was transpiring between people. His life must have been a terrible mystery and frustration to him. Was he capable of loving us? It didn't seem so. Was he the carrier of a mental illness? I have long since made my peace with him.

Sometime later that day, I drove over to see Sandra, who had moved into a small house near us on Crescent Island. I was worried; when I'd spoken with her that morning, she had seemed depressed. I was exhausted as I drove back. As I headed through our gate, I noticed a car behind me. It was my father in his open Cadillac convertible. He followed me into the parking lot next to me. I got out of my car.

"Millicent! Millicent! Come talk to me!"

I didn't turn my head, just shook it and walked away, his voice trailing after me, "Millicent, Millicent . . ."

I never saw him again. He died two years later while having dinner with his sister in his mother's house. I wonder sometimes what he might have said.

About two months after he died, there was a terrible hurricane, the worst one in many years. I remember looking out my window and down the beach where I could see the quay and his house. I thought I caught a glimpse of him standing there against the storm. The house was almost completely destroyed. Some said he came back and cleansed it. Phil McPhee said the only thing left in the living room and still hanging on the wall was a portrait of his mother and me.

29

White Rams and Laughing Seagulls

According to Jung, "the island is the refuge from the menacing assault of the 'sea' of the unconscious—an area of metaphysical force where the forces of 'immense illogic' are distilled. The island is also a symbol of death."

During these years we came to understand that although Sandra's illness might have good periods, it would, for the most part, cast a desperate shadow over all of us. But the island provided an antidote and I took advantage of it. It helped me to put my father and Sandra into perspective— like nature itself—and I would walk for hours all over the island.

On the day of the spring solstice, I decided to walk to Cove Island, which, with its breakwater, formed a harbor between the two islands. I had made careful plans, for I needed to be alone. It was long trip across the breakwater, which could only be crossed at low tide. Packing a simple picnic, I made my way down across the dunes to the beach. Wild roses in purples and pinks bordered the dunes and shiny sea grass slithered in the breeze and the warm sun. The early morning sun splashed across the wet beach until all the stones sparkled.

As everyone who lives by the sea knows, gulls are the souls of dead sailors, and if you should hear the sound of a laughing gull you know you have come across the spirit of an old sea captain. I met with such a fellow that morning on Crescent Island. I was looking out over the island's tidal pools, struck by the pulsing of the waves, my ears roaring and my poor spirit longing to join the dance . . . and then the litany of whys started—*Why? Why can't I understand? Why is there suffering? Why must our child suffer? Why am I here witnessing this? Why am I so often in so much pain, so much endless mourning?*

That's when the old sailor appeared in the guise of a seagull, for those questions always attract him. He circled slowly over my head, wings arched to float on the breeze . . . and he laughed. *Ha ha*, then *Ha ha* again from the very depths of his crusty old soul. I was furious and feeling foolish for being mocked, so I shouted at him. He wasn't impressed, and circled about me laughing a few more times before gliding off.

The full moon had sucked the tide back from the edges of the beach, and I was able to walk easily on the moist sand until I came to the tip of the island and climbed up the path, through the long light-green grass worn down by the sheep that made their home there. When I reached the top of the steep meadow, I stopped to look about. The field stretched for a mile or so on either side and was rimmed by a forest of green pine and tall leafy trees and bisected by the sensuous curve of a stone wall. Great white fluffs of sheep grazed like little fallen clouds across the meadow. The fields rolling down to the ocean looked like the Scottish Highlands or the island of Orpheus, a place that had been bewitched by his song.

Beyond this the island gave way to secret caves with hidden beaches and jagged cliffs hanging over the sea. I was so overwhelmed by the feeling of harmony and magic that had it not been for years of civilization in my blood, I would have fallen on my knees and worshipped.

I made my way to the central point and focus of my walk. It was a small island surrounded by black seawater and overlooked by a cliff. I was uncomfortably aware of being watched, stared at. I looked around for the intruder, and then I saw him poised at the very brink of his small island with such enormous dignity and stillness that he could have stood on that spot for a millennium. His large horns curved around his head in a half circle like the crown of an ancient god. The proud head looked foreboding and powerful. He stood there motionless, his coat luminous in the sun. His dignity rang out against the black rocks and tough pines and out across the sea. Except for a slight shudder, I stood as motionless as he.

It is impossible to stay in a sacred place too long. Eventually I turned my back and walked slowly away.

The path now led into the pines, across soft brown needles, past orange butterflies, rare black terns with yellow heads and white marks down their backs, blood red poison berries with shining leaves. It led into a circle of leafy trees where I stood swimming in flashing strobes of new green light. I stood among the elm, oak, maple, and tamarack, each grand tree singing a different tune through its new leaves. The elms sang a sharp song that flew away into a scherzo or fugue. The large oak slowly repeated its low, heavy bass tunes. The tamarack sang its melody of harps and hollow wood. The poplar was always my favorite. Today I thought I heard it laughing, its green-and-silver fluttering a delicate whisper of joy. I heard that joy on that spring solstice, even though I knew the poplar is a symbol of pain and lamentation thought to grow in the underworld with its foliage trembling in the least breath of air.

I walked on to the spot where I intended to eat my meal and watch the full moon grow out of the sea from the east as the huge orange sun was falling into the water in the west.

The spell was finally broken and soon the forest had

black corners. I turned and made my way home across the breakwater. There in the moon path, the questions that had started the day returned, buzzing in my head—*Isn't it enough to have just enjoyed the day? Why does Sandra have to suffer so—why do we? Is there no peace? Where is God?*

It was then that I heard the soft flapping of wings again, folding around my head. I looked up to hear him answer . . .

Ha ha ha ha ha, he laughed, *Ha ha ha*.

30

D. C.

In 1982, two years after my surgery, Bobby and I left Crescent Island to spend some time in Washington, D.C. Before we left, Bobby had bought Sandra, when she was twenty-five, a beautiful large house with a tower, surrounded by the ocean on two sides, a little pond, fields, and access to a small visible beach. It was about six miles from Crescent Island and she seemed happy to have her own home.

Bobby had been offered several jobs in Washington and ended up working for the then vice president, George H. W. Bush, in the Old Executive Office Building next to the White House, where the vice president's office was. We both felt it was good to get away from all the complications at home, and I started working with Jerome Bernstein, a Jungian analyst, which was to prove a great blessing.

Angus and his wife, Emma, joined us with their two children; he was going to George Mason to study arbitration. It was a happy and special time for all of us, exploring Washington and the countryside and meeting new people. I was involved with the Washington Ballet, took classes every day, and wrote a libretto called "The Witches of Salem" that was performed at the Kennedy Center. I was always interested in the subject of women accused of causing harm to children, and their fate.

Sandra came to visit occasionally. Sometimes everything went fairly well, and sometimes it didn't. Often we wouldn't hear from her for months, as she refused to speak to us—me especially. We all went home in the summer and for holidays.

During our last year in D.C.—about three years after Sandra moved into her new house—we got a call in Washington from a woman whom we had met at Sandra's on one of our visits back to Maine. She called to tell us that Sandra was depressed, and we guessed drinking, which was very bad news. They had a cousin named Joey who was connected with an organization in their Catholic church that helped people. They felt he should move in with her and help her—we said fine, and so he did. Joey moved in and seemed to be a great help.

We went home to the island for Thanksgiving and Sandra called to ask if Joey could join the family for Thanksgiving dinner. Sandra arrived at the house followed by Joey, who was wearing a shiny white suit, a black tie, black shoes, and gold rings and bracelets. I saw Grandma's eyebrows shoot up as she saw him, she being dressed in her good Boston tweed suit with a silk scarf and heavy, sturdy brown shoes. I couldn't help but smile a little. I seated Joey next to me at dinner.

"So, Joey, tell me about yourself."

Joey didn't miss a beat. "Yeah, I'm a member of the New York Mafia. My brother carries the gun and the money, not me, and my father just shot up a store that was giving us trouble."

"You won't believe this, Joey," I said, "but we have something in common—fathers who shoot at things." Joey looked surprised. "You see, my father had an eye for the ladies and one night at a big party he was giving"—I pointed down the beach—"he found a lovely blonde lady and wanted to take her out on his boat. So he went down to the dock, lady in tow, and rang the bell. No response on the boat. He went and got the jeep and honked the horn—no response. He was getting upset. Still holding onto the lady, he got his gun out and proceeded to shoot the boat. The captain and the first mate thought they were back in World War II—it woke them up." I wasn't about to let Joey think we were a bunch of patsies.

Joey stayed with Sandra for about two years. The second year, he bought a trailer to live in and put two pink flamingos on either side of his door.

One day, when Bobby and I were back in Washington, we looked at each other and decided that, although we enjoyed the glitter and politics of Washington, it was time to go home to Crescent Island. Angus, Emma, and the children moved back and built a house next door to ours. I was to go home to get our old house ready—it was full of mold, had faulty electricity, and was generally in poor shape. Bobby was going to Australia for ten days.

Tom, who ran our tree nursery, picked me up at the airport. It was a freezing cold day in January with a foot and a half of snow on the ground. As our lotus gate slowly opened, I passed through a shadow and wondered if I would be truly able to return home and felt a strong sense of foreboding around Sandra.

The gate closed behind us and we went up the hill. As we turned the corner, spread out before us was the place I loved more dearly than any place on earth—and I had traveled to many places. A tall stand of tamarind trees stood on one side of the hill—out beyond them lay the Atlantic Ocean, sparkling and still in the windless, freezing day. How I had missed that ocean. I felt a rush of joy and hope that I could live here now.

As I arrived at the house, Ling-Ling, our little black-and-white shih tzu, jumped off my lap to explore. Phyllis, Chris, and Ed were all at the front door to greet us. Phyllis, then in her seventies, grew up on the farm and knew more about our family than one person should. I called her my nana. Chris, who worked at the tree nursery, had come up to the house to help move us back in and brought Ed, who helped out part-time. They were a welcoming and reassuring sight.

I looked around at the piles of boxes and furniture and decided to wait a while before tackling them.

Phyllis was planning to stay. When I went to bed I opened a book of poems by Rumi, the thirteenth-century mystic. The book opened to these lines:

> *The moment you accept what troubles*
> *You've been given, the door opens.*

I went to sleep to the sounds of the sea.

31

Fire

When I awoke the next morning, the temperature was well below freezing and turned out to be a record low. The sea smoke (caused by the sea being warmer than the air) was pouring out of the ocean and reaching up to some twenty feet. It was fascinating to watch, and as I did, the mist turned into huge Spanish galleons racing each other to the end of the island and then disappearing.

Chris, Phyllis, and I started opening the boxes and unpacking. Phyllis was planning to be with me that night but she looked tired, so I told her to go home and take the day off. She and Chris went home and I attempted to take Ling-Ling for a walk. The cold had hardened the snow on top, so you couldn't walk on it without stamping one footprint out at a time—a wet, cold, hard job—and the road was sheer ice, so Ling-Ling didn't get much of a walk.

When I went in, I dropped my parka and boots by the side door. I tried to sort out the mail, a job I always dreaded as it meant more work, made a little supper, and locked myself in the house. I soon realized the furnace couldn't keep up with the cold and the house was freezing. It was an old and rather dreary house. I found myself wishing the McPhees were still with us, but they had retired to Canada, and Sadie, who had been with us for some twenty years, had died some years ago. I had forgotten to check if Bobby's sister and brother-in-law, who lived across the field, were home or had gone away, as they often did, for a few weeks or a weekend. If so, the nearest neighbor was two and a half miles away and I was alone in an empty house surrounded by pitch blackness.

I wasn't happy to be alone. As it got dark, the old fear started that I might just see a glimpse of Mother behind a curtain or sitting dead still in a dark room. I flew up the stairs with Ling-Ling in my arms and bolted the brass locks shut. I took Ling-Ling under the covers with me because it was so cold. She always lies so still and provides a little warm spot. As I fell asleep, I could hear the loud banging and groaning of the tree limbs as the cold cracked and split them.

Sometime during the night I was woken up by a persistent smothered ticking. I thought it was my alarm clock and put my pillow over my head. It was cold and I was too tired to deal with it. Suddenly there was a loud explosion and the sound of breaking glass. I woke up and lay in bed furious, thinking it must be a burglar. I was seldom fearful in a real emergency or danger. When I opened my eyes, I slowly understood the room was full of smoke—flames were shooting up outside the large sliding-glass doors on the terrace.

I fumbled for the telephone—it was dead—then, without slippers or bathrobe, I grabbed Ling-Ling, took a large breath through the blanket, and headed for the door. I knew nothing about fires—I didn't know how dangerous it could have been to open the door to the hall, and I didn't know the fire alarms overhead were melting and dripping from the heat. With one arm around Ling-Ling and the other feeling along the wall, as the smoke was so thick, I found the stairs. At that point I had to breathe. I let my breath out and when I drew it back in, I can remember thinking, *My lungs feel hot.* I reached the side door, opened it, and kicked my boots and parka outside. I put them on and started across the field. It was like walking in one of those nightmares where you can't get anywhere—I had to stamp out each step in the crusty snow and kept falling down. Poor Ling-Ling must have been squeezed and bumped, but she never complained.

I kept yelling "Fire!" to no one in particular, as it was 4:00 A.M. and my sister and brother-in-law were either fast asleep or not home. When I reached their house, I called the fire department and woke up Nate, Bobby's nephew, who was home for a visit, and we stamped back to the house and watched helplessly until the fire department came. The town fire department managed to get through the gates and down the icy roads, but everything, including the pond, was frozen over, so they used water from their truck. The fire department from Scarborough went in the wrong gate and got lost in the woods; the back roads were treacherous. But in the end they all made it to the house. The only things I asked them to save were a portrait of Bobby's grandmother—a museum piece—and my portrait. The only other things I would have hated to lose were photographs, but I had made duplicates of all my favorite ones of the children, sisters, and brothers and given them to various members of the family.

The chief of police arrived, and I watched the mostly volunteer fire department go in and out of the house, which had turned completely black from soot and smoke. Tom, Chris, and Ed arrived and we all hugged. The fire chief informed me that in another three minutes I would have been dead from smoke inhalation.

The house hadn't burned down, but the fire had incinerated the basement and burst through the first floor and everything was smoke-damaged. We decided to tear it down and move into our small guesthouse, which we had just built. It was only one room, two burners for a kitchen, and a moldy bathroom. Rather than rent a house for the two years we thought it would take to build a house, we added a bedroom and bath and fixed the kitchen. It was enjoyable and simple living in that small space by the sea.

It took three years to build and furnish the house the way we wanted it. Looking back on the fire, I suppose it was another invitation from death, although I believe the long, slow death of love in childhood was the worst.

32

Sandra, Marriage & Child

We had settled down to building a new house. Sandra appeared to have been doing all right with Joey, but he left around this time. She was sitting on the dunes one day, playing the guitar and singing. She had the most beautiful, haunting voice. A young man called Derrick was rowing back from Cove Island, where he had been living alone for some three years, with the job of keeping an eye on it. He saw her and fell in love. He was a professional musician—guitar was his specialty. The next surprising call we got was the news that they were going to be married and at the last minute we were invited. It was a simple family wedding and we were so happy for Sandra.

Sandra soon became pregnant. They fixed up their house, made an office and apartment out of the garage and a lovely room for the baby. We were with Sandra in the hospital when the baby was born, a beautiful dark-haired child—a girl. Sandra was happy. Derrick helped with the baby they called Sidra and worked with Sandra on her book about her time at McLean. They were happy.

At our thirty-fifth wedding anniversary, Sandra got up and made a toast:

> *I wanted to say a couple of things . . . If I can remember them . . . I flunked public speaking . . . Essentially: that I love my parents very much, that they are unique and incredible people. I know everyone knows that but I wanted to say that I felt this and that I am very*

proud of them. There are times that are most special to me. Like last night when my great big father was standing on the dance floor looking handsome in front of more than five hundred people, waiting for my very beautiful mother to come dance with him. Those are the times that touch me the deepest, that are most special. They seem like two kids wrapped up and protected forever, in eternal love. Lastly I have a challenge to these two. I figured if I made it a request they wouldn't respond as well. These two seem to need a challenge. My challenge is that they make it another thirty-five years to their seventieth aniversary. They will only be around ninety then, so they will have no excuse not to meet the challenge. Of course, they'll need their family and friends here with them—so all of you are challenged too . . .

In the first four years after Sidra's birth, things went tolerably well between Sandra and us. Derrick and Sandra adored Sidra, and we got together in Florida and on Crescent Island with Angus and Emma and their children. I felt very happy and relieved. At last we had a family.

About five years into their marriage, things started to go wrong. I began to feel a sense of dread, as if I had a notion of things to come. I don't know what started the downward cycle.

Then came a bad period. I suggested to Sandra that we do some therapy together by phone, as Jerome Bernstein, my Jungian analyst, had moved to Santa Fe. It did not go well. I still felt too guilty and every phone session ended with me in tears after I hung up. I had to stop. Sandra began drinking and the telephone calls started. Hurtful and vicious, they were to continue for many years. Inevitably a call would come in the middle of the night, and she would be full of rage and accusations. The calls went all over Maine, across the country and abroad. One night she asked us to take her to McLean. We all drove down and arrived at 2:00 P.M. They wouldn't take her.

Sometimes the calls were to a friend whose husband was dying. Sandra would announce that she was sleeping with her husband.

Sometimes the calls were to my dance company. Once, in the office, the business manager, Annie, answered the phone to hear a woman screaming at her, "Millicent is nothing but a rich bitch who has destroyed the dance company; everyone knows it! Can she dance?"

"Yes, she is a beautiful dancer," Annie replied, turning pale.

"It's okay, Annie," I said. "I believe I know who it is. It's okay." I didn't want her to know I was stunned too.

There was a call to her trustee, who had refused a request for money. "How would you like to find your little dog dead?"

Sometimes Bobby and I got as many as six or eight calls a day and calls at all hours of the night until we were unnerved and exhausted and took the phone off the hook. We also got calls from others she'd harassed as though we could do something to stop them.

It was around this time that Sandra and Derrick began having serious problems. Sandra's drinking didn't help. The McPhees often came down from Canada for the summers, as they had retired, and we all tried to help her keep up the household, which now included one cat, four dogs, and eight ferrets. But in spite of her good resolve, things kept getting worse. The dining table was so full of junk that no one could eat off it. Since she didn't need to eat, Sandra felt Sidra didn't need to eat either. It was all reminiscent of Lucy.

Derrick and Sandra got a divorce and divided Sidra's time between them. When Sidra was about twelve, Sandra lost custody of her and Sidra went to live with her dad.

One day we received the following letter:

> . . . *I began more and more to realize how my parents felt about me; how they had always treated me and that they weren't going to have understanding or compassion or behave decently or truthfully towards me.*
>
> *I had never ever been suicidal until that point in my life. Being desperate for justice, I, at times, began to seriously contemplate killing myself in my parents' bed, leaving a note that read, Here it began and here it ends. May God bring justice to you for what you have done to me. I'd have shot my brains out, so it would be messy—like my life had been. So, maybe, they'd finally get what they had done because they could clearly see my insides now. —Sandra*

Bobby's words rang in my ears: "A life sentence for us all."

33

Last Visit to Cumberland Island

The horse was lying drowned in about four feet of water, and as the waves gently moved him, he performed a weird dance in slow motion as if he were galloping in death. It was to be our last visit to Cumberland. We had come down the inland waterway on a chartered boat, past the slews, towns, and inlets that spread out to the sea in the warm spring weather. We landed at the Greyfields dock, where the family had turned the grand house into an inn some fifteen years earlier.

My sister, who still lived on the island but had left for the summer, had loaned us a car, a hard thing to come by on the island now, as the Park Service only let island people have them. We drove right to the beach down ten miles of road, with little armadillos running for cover and the palms creating dizzy shadows of light and dark on the white oyster-shell road, to be greeted by the galloping horse in the waves. We continued down the beach until we found the road through the dunes to Stafford. I noticed something in the bushes on the side of the road. It was a group of backpackers. I was startled. I had never seen anyone on the road, and it brought the realization back to me that the Park Service, which had taken over much of the island when Jimmy Carter was president, had allowed campers and day visitors, and had also killed off the wild boar and alligators.

We arrived at Stafford and stopped. It was guarded by a large, ghastly, completely bone-white tree. Stafford looked even more dilapidated than I remembered it, although later my niece was to fix it up and live in it, as the Park Service couldn't afford to take it.

I sat looking at the large plantation house, remembering for some reason my grandmother dressed beautifully in soft flowing peach in the little green room where she arranged flowers, my grandfather napping on a couch or playing golf, the terrible rotten-egg smell of the supposedly healthy sulfur water, and the beautiful bedrooms with peach silk blanket covers and the letter *C* embroidered on them. I decided I wanted to remember it the way it was in my childhood and didn't go in. We left Stafford to go down the short drive to where my sister now lives, and where Mother had lived in the small house Sean had built. Again we drove by the vultures sitting on the stark branches of dead trees like some hideous black-feathered disease while the large roots of trees crept and struggled across the road.

We had a picnic by the pool—I remembered, when I was about twelve, my mother killing a water moccasin on the edge of the pool with a garden hoe, while I watched in terror and wondered if I had been swimming with it in the pool's murky green water. Nate, who had taken care of Mother before she died, lived to help out my sister and was still singing to his pots and pans. When he died, my sister arranged for the funeral in the little church where John Kennedy was to be married. The tears streamed down her face.

We made our way to Plum Orchard, which was to my mind the most beautiful of all the houses: with low, white marble steps leading up to a terrace and tall pillars which led to an entrance of lovely French doors and windows—a magnificent white mansion. All the family had gone now and the soul of the house had fled with them, leaving the windows looking like the empty eyes of a skull.

At the end of our visit, we drove over to see Mother's and Jack's graves, only to find the family had put a tall locked fence around them to keep the public out. I stood there for a while under the old, gnarled oaks that were casting shadows on the graves and thought, *How ironic and sad—there is still no way to reach her.*

The story about the end of Dungeness goes that Aunt Fergie and her manager loved to stalk poachers, and with her knife at her side and their guns in hand, they would go poacher hunting. On this particular night they found a group of them laughing and drinking. They snuck up, took a couple of shots, and unfortunately wounded one badly. The poachers fled but they came back to avenge their friend. First they shot the island boat full of holes, tied the steering wheel, and set it out to sea. Then they set about burning down Dungeness. Some of the family arrived in time to see it in flames and later said, "There was nothing we could do but watch it burn. The heat and flames were fierce." All that was left in the end were some walls and the tall, black, burnt tower protesting against the sky.

The Park Service had placed a stand at the top of the stone stairs, leading to nowhere, with a picture of my mother's wedding, which startled me. My father stood, slim and handsome, beside her. It felt strange and intrusive to me, but then I felt maybe she had left her picture there to leave her stamp and spirit on her beloved Dungeness.

We left the island shortly after that.

There are still relatives who love and enjoy it and find there a delightful community in each other and carry on with many of the pleasures of the past. Angus and Emma and the grandchildren still go, and love it. But for me, Cumberland Island is an incredibly beautiful island in which the past has decayed and gone. The island that sustained my mother has vanished. It is now part of my history, the past and grand memories – my mother's island.

I sat in the bow of the boat as we left, feeling as if something or someone I treasured had died. I watched that beautiful and enchanted island until it disappeared over the horizon. I will not return.

34

A Dream and a Father's Funeral on Crescent Island

Many years after my father died, I dreamed about him and remembered his funeral as if it had just taken place. In the dream I pounded and pushed on the front door of my father's house—the door was huge and made of heavy, dark wood. It gave way, and I found myself standing on the redbrick floor in front of the fireplace. Father came down the stairs and approached as if he didn't see me.

I reached for the long antique bronze poker on the edge of the fireplace. It was shaped somewhat like a harpoon. With one terrible movement that felt like slow motion, I thrust the poker straight through him—straight through his heart. He fell backward on the brick. I looked carefully at his body to make sure the poker was in the proper place; to kill such a villain takes proper magic—to kill a vampire the poker must pierce the heart.

Out of the corner of my eye, I saw an animal. A small fox appeared out of the dining room, ran the length of the hall, and disappeared out the front door. I turned quickly and reached for an old antique birdcage, which had hung in the hall since I could remember. There was no bird to sing behind its bars. Grasping it carefully in both arms, I turned and quickly followed the fox out the front door.

This fantasy or half dream, which seemed as real to me as any other reality I have known, now was very much on my mind as I dressed for my father's funeral. From that dream and that anger, I eventually had to face the fact that I was capable of murder. I had to face that shadow and claim back what as a little girl I'd lost.

After that dream I reminisced about his funeral. It was a small country funeral held in a white oilcan church on the edge of Crescent Farm overlooking a large salt marsh and cemetery. It had seemed appropriate to me to wear black. I wondered what my sisters would wear. It was cold and wet.

The church was filled. We were a bit late. Maybe it was my imagination, but as I walked in, I thought I heard a ripple from the back section where the old Crescent Farm caretaker and all those who had worked on the farm over the years were sitting. As I had chosen not to talk with my father over the past years, I had seen little of them. Suddenly Red, the farm manager, stepped out of a booth laughing and pumped my hand. I was startled but nodded in what could be described as a civilized manner.

The church seating was a masterpiece of discretion. Three wives had produced eleven assorted children—step, half, and whole—and they all were there, except Mother. They had to be placed discreetly, as they were not known for their self-discipline.

The latest marriage had produced three stepsisters. They were all blonde and beautiful and had been seen from time to time riding horseback behind their stepfather in an appreciative and loving manner. They sat together on the left side of the church—their heads covered by silk scarves, which gave them the appearance of English royalty.

I saw Sandra come in and stand back in the back as I turned to watch my eldest brother escort the third wife down the aisle. I could hear his earlier words of frustration with our father ringing in my head, but after Father's death, my brother (and his wife) did everything they could to heal our family. I admired him for that.

The congregation was suddenly hushed and all one could

hear was the September storm pelting the sides of the church. Slowly the coffin was carried down the aisle—it was too heavy a burden for its bearers; as it reached the front of the church, right at the elbow of my older sister, one of the bearers let his corner drop. I may have imagined the body thumped against the side of the coffin in a last furious protest, but everyone heard my sister clearly, in an almost hysterical laugh, cry out, "Oh my God, don't drop him in my lap!" and squeeze back into her pew.

And so began the inglorious and peculiar funeral of our father. The minister spoke honestly about him. I could feel the tension mounting, but I was determined not to give those endless peeping glares of the gathered audience a clue as to my feelings.

Finally came the Lord's Prayer. That terrible desire to laugh aloud that had attacked my sister now rose up in my throat as I rephrased the Lord's Prayer in a loud whisper:

"Our Father who art in heaven—thank God, thank God."

I couldn't remember what Goethe said about the consequence of thoughts fantasized or committed, but I knew instinctively they were grave and bowed my head in prayer.

Part Three

35

Northern Island

In the Vedic tradition, life falls into three parts: "first the child and mother, second work, family and play, third the elders go into the forest to explore the spiritual life."

On the island far to the north near the Canadian border, all the lines are straight with cathedral pines; dark, jagged rocks form its circumference; and sharp, pristine, crystal light illuminates what hides. There is a small outdoor chapel, whose old wooden cross leans to the north. The ocean's horizon curves slightly as it falls toward the white plains of the north wind. This is the island of the patriarchs, whose faces are like its granite rocks. In 1807 my husband's family acquired Northern Island. It became part of our story by my marriage to Bobby. This island does not have many animals, but it is filled with birds. It is the island of the spirit. It is here that the birds soar in the first and last light of day. It is where we will be buried.

Northern Island floats on the curved edge of a cold sea near the Bay of Fundy. It rushes away from the mainland, leaving only a thin black line behind. The low tide drops fifteen feet, pulling the sea water out of the coves and bays. One has to wait till it fills them up and lifts the boats to land or load. Black cliffs guard one side of the island's bay; the other side gives way to stone and sand beaches and fields. In the spring, the North Wind retreats to her throne of ice, leaving a cool summer breeze warmed by the sun and a promise to return. She leaves behind her light, which is crystal clear like the light of halos and icicles. It has a mysterious quality about it—as if in its clarity, nature is giving a clue: the only reason for being here is to search for the light that comes with enlightenment that comes with halos, the light within, the light that appears when you cross over and go behind the north wind.

Here is an island civilized by a thoughtful male energy. On this island, life is simple and quiet, and nature keeps presenting its bounty and gifts. The rocks on the beaches are rolled smooth by the sea, small, exquisite sea sculptures, black rocks with white rings considered lucky, olive-green ones in odd shapes, small pure-white ones, and ones that appear to have some strange hieroglyphic message on them.

Sometimes the fog rolls in over the bay, beaches, docks, and houses and tactile things vanish, as if they were never there in the first place, an illusion. The island almost seems to breathe when the wind passes through the long green pine needles, sighing and singing. It is an island of music with the hum of lobster boats, the foghorn, water lapping on the rocks and beaches or booming against the cliffs, the bell buoy in the distance, and the birdsong and crickets chirping.

It is also an island of silence on a summer night when the north wind is blowing in other places, when the night sky creates a huge dome with a million stars and the aurora borealis flashes across in brilliant colors, and you can hear the silence of falling stars.

The island is shaped like an H and is twenty-five miles in circumference. In the arms of the eastern side of the H is a mile-long beach, curved like a crescent moon with cliffs on one side and dunes in the middle, with tall sea grass that moves in waves to meet the pines and spruce at the end of a field. Across the freezing cold water, the beach looks out on three small islands called The Brothers. Watching and seeing all this pristine beauty, one feels surrounded by the painted strokes of a Zen master.

There is a two-mile dirt road that you can bump along in an old truck or jeep to the beach, or you can walk miles of trails. Some paths wander along the island's edge, where you pass the inlets, coves, or open sea; others lead up steep banks of rocks with Indian stone piles giving directions, which lead to magnificent views of the beach and fields. Sometimes on an old path, you have to crawl through a dark tunnel of underbrush and dead branches that scratch and claw and make it easy to get lost.

Other smaller islands surround Northern Island on one side and create estuaries that Indians still canoed down when Bobby was young. Their dark, quiet rivers are one of the most magic and beautiful realms of the island. The tall spruce trees were once used for masts on boats and brigantines. In one of the inlets an occasional eagle's nest can be seen, and just outside the estuary seals stretch out on the rocks.

Northern Island has a chapel with an old wooden moss-covered cross leaning slightly to the north, logs for the choir and congregation, and the bay stretching out as a backdrop. It is a peaceful, sacred place to be quiet or meditate. The light pours slanted through the cathedral pines as if giving its blessing. No intermediary here—just a log to sit on in a quiet space with a quiet mind.

There have been marriages and christenings there, as well as Sunday morning services conducted by Bobby's father or relatives from the past. Sometimes in my mind's eye, when the rain and fog drip from the trees and tap on the forest floor, I can hear my reserved father-in-law—long since passed away—laughing and tap-dancing through the forest. I am glad to see him so happy.

Overlooking the bay, a graveyard has recently been built by Beth, Bobby's sister, on top of a hill behind the houses. It is formed in a circle out of the island stone with a simple gate at its entrance. It is the first stamp of feminine influence on island ground that has been dominated by the patriarchs.

Sometimes in the night, when all the boundaries dissipate, I can feel the island float away through the inlets and estuaries, through the dark, calm water shining with stars. It floats slowly away to the northern end of the sea and I am back in my dream, in the dark hull of my boat, sitting and swaying on my cross, listening for what I thought was the voice of God.

I never really leave the island. I take it with me, its music and its silence. I go through the fields of crickets and trails of green moss, smell the strong scent of pine, hear the water lapping on the shore, and see the stars in the night sky. I imagine the white half-moon beach in the northern light, and sit quietly on my log in the chapel, facing the tilting cross.

36

Sidra, Northern Island, and the Cross

Out beyond ideas of wrong-doing and right-doing
There is a field
I'll meet you there
—Rumi

It was late August and the smell of autumn was in the air when Sidra, now fifteen, Bobby, and I got on the boat to go to Northern Island. Sidra and I went to the front of the boat to lie on our stomachs in the warm sun and watch the boat cut through the blue sea.

We landed and were greeted by the manager and a few relatives. We threw our luggage into the old truck and walked up the hill to the big yellow house with our very old Ling-Ling and our new shih tzu puppies, Ping Pong and Shiva—Shiva being well named after the god of destruction and dance, as he was inclined to bite. We had a delicious dinner of island vegetables and lamb and went to bed early.

The next morning, as was my habit, I rose at around 5:00 and crept downstairs to the hammock under the large wraparound veranda. The view down the hill, which poured itself into the bay, was magnificent. An early morning fog lifted slowly off the still water. It was quiet, as the birds hadn't woken up yet to sing. The only sound was the occasional moan of a loon.

I meditated quietly and moved into that place of tremendous peace. I thought of what I had asked the Maharishi Mahesh Yogi, if meditating were a small death, and I wondered now if by meditating one moved toward the spirit and away from the body to that peaceful space of stillness which holds death, my childhood fascination.

Just before the morning light appears over the bay, there is a moment of silence, when every living creature is still. The trees stop rattling. The pendulum stops at the base of the curve. Enchantment happens. I sat there swaying in the hammock, neither joyful nor sad, but feeling connected for a few precious moments with the immense beauty around me, tears flowing down my face because of the gentle morning breeze.

Sometime after the sun had risen, Sidra came clattering out on the porch and joined me on the hammock, swinging it a wee bit wildly from side to side. I looked at my beautiful fifteen-year-old granddaughter, long black hair, blue eyes, a dancer's body.

"Sidra, could we go sit on a log in the chapel?"

"Sure."

We walked together down to the chapel and sat on one of the logs, facing the weather-beaten cross that leans to the north.

"You know, many people have come here to talk about things they might not otherwise speak of. You're a little young to hear all of this." I paused. "Just know that you are a good person, and many people and your mom love you. Your mom gave us a wonderful granddaughter." I reached over and touched her on the arm and gave her a hug. The little girl who wears a cross around her neck, sings in the Pentecostal choir, loves to dance and write, and has a lovely, pure singing voice—she had already been through so much. I worried that she might be slowly defeated. Her middle name is Millicent.

"You've been given beauty, a very good brain, and talent in the arts. Sometimes it seems to me everyone is given different tasks and gifts, and I hope so much that the arts, music, and the life of the spirit we both care about will always be there for you."

Sidra turned and looked up at me and said, "I hope so too."

"There is something else I do, which is helpful and kind of funny. When my dad, your great-grandfather, died, we hadn't gotten along too well, and he died before we could talk. So I sat on this log and closed my eyes and conjured him up and asked him to come sit on the log and talk, and he did, and eventually we made our peace together. You can go back into your dreams too, you know, and talk to people.

"So Sidra, if you ever need to talk to your mom, and you can't reach her, bring her here in your mind's eye and talk to her. I think you'll be amazed at what she says. Know that I will always, always be here for you, and remember that you will always be my pumpkin, my butterfly. Sidra—my star-child."

Sidra didn't say much except "I know, Nona, I know. Thank you for telling me this." She got up and went over to the cross and gave it a slight nudge, as if to straighten it, but it stayed stubbornly leaning to the north. That was alright, she is under the protection of the cross, as I was. Then she turned and smiled.

37

Overwhelmed: The Next Years on Crescent Island

It was one day in the year 2000 that I fell facedown on the uneven brick in the center of town, and lay in a pool of blood. Four hours later, I woke in the emergency room to see Bobby and Angus standing at the foot of my bed. It had started in phases—at first, my muscles would quickly and unexpectedly give out and I would be suddenly very dizzy. I would fall always facedown—stairs became a misery, as I was losing my depth perception and becoming confused. My left arm and shoulder were very painful. Ripples of depression and exhaustion started. I hadn't left the house in months except to go to the grocery store or out with Bobby. The day I fell on the brick sidewalk, I knew I shouldn't go into town, but I was determined to get Bobby a seventieth birthday present and have lunch with Angus, who wanted to talk about my health.

It began in modern dance classes and rehearsals—I couldn't get up off the floor when a dance piece required floor work. I stopped taking class. The depletion of my energy became such that I couldn't manage or cope with the company, and even music could not release the desire to move. Soon after that, I closed my company of thirty-five years. I felt terribly for the company, but I couldn't cope with Sandra's continuing anger, the problems it created for her and for Bobby and I, and the dance company.

I resumed working regularly with Jerome, visiting with him in Santa Fe and having a recurrent dream. He had said several times, "Be careful you both don't drown." In the repeating dream about Sandra, I am drowning, sinking, arms and legs floating and weaving about me in a helpless, macabre dance . . . drowning weightless and numb on the tides . . . soft, white, porous skin becoming sponge-like . . . arms reaching out to Sandra as she sinks below me with her heavy rage . . . razors floating slowly by . . . I'm sinking into deeper water which is pressing on my brain and I can do nothing, brain sopped, drowning, needing breath . . . we are floating helplessly downward.

For the next three years, things got worse for Sandra and for all of us—her drinking didn't help. The family learned how to prevent her phone calls, in which Sandra would, in her brilliance and intuition, say things that were indelibly wounding. While drinking she called one family member and said she was going to show a friend who was in a psychiatric ward how to use a razor so she could properly cut her wrist. The telephone became her umbilical cord to the world, her lonely world.

She called newspapers, acquaintances, and friends, describing to them how we had destroyed her. I wasn't surprised when, years later, a lady said to me, "I'm surprised you aren't the monster I thought you were." (She had been a regular recipient of Sandra's calls.)

There were endless attacks from her lawyers demanding money. She took to stalking at night, parking in front of people's houses to scare them. This went on for five or six years, while Sidra was in her teens. We finally were forced to take out restraining orders. In my late sixties, I took Celexa and Wellbutrin until I couldn't stand their effect any longer. Bobby took me to the Mayo Clinic. I was so disoriented and unsteady that without Bobby's help I could not have made it to my appointments. After two weeks, the diagnosis was trauma and stress, both recent and from my childhood. They could offer no help—no solution.

One night, lying in bed and listening to the ocean and the light rain, I was numb except for wisps of depression, and I heard Bobby's words again, "It's a life sentence for all of us," in the rush of the ocean and the falling rain before I fell asleep and dreamed.

We have gone before the judge who has pronounced us guilty, of exactly what is unclear. We ourselves are the judge, the jury, and the jailors. Life imprisonment—a life sentence. The bars of the jail cover many acres in my dream. The western side is sunny much of the time, but beyond that there is a rim of blackness. The tormentor lives there and sometimes comes out of the dark and joins us. Sometimes we play poker—no one wins, but sometimes a burnt smell floats out from the darkness and we hear a slow, primitive growling, a sound so low and deadly that we cover our ears and press against the bars. There is no gate. I press against the bed, and the bars feel like human bones and sinews, strong and stiff.

I wrote in my journal:

> *Sandra, I have to let you go now. I am drowning in sleep and being strangled by my muscles and it's painful. I'm getting old, and I have not been well for some time. My darling, I wanted a daughter so badly, so very badly, and I have loved you so much and I hope and pray that maybe someday our passage here won't always be an unhealed wound for both of us.*
>
> *There have been times when I have lost my very strong belief in and connection to the spiritual life because you have suffered so much and because we have all suffered from something none of us knows how to heal. It is dangerous for me to lose my connection*

to the other side—and to not be moved by music and dance. When nature loses its healing magic and becomes a dull grey, I struggle not to drown.

It's been a long time since I have taken dance class, but I know in time my muscles will release me to dance again and sleep will be where I rest and create and not drown. I will find enormous pleasure in each day and be thankful for all the beauty and love that surrounds me. And I will miss, so much, that for now, we can't take a walk on the beach or share a poem—share our lives.

Some time later when Bobby and I received the book Sandra was writing, we found the following poem:

Forgiveness

I want to tell you
what I believe
about forgiveness.
It is a state
of consciousness
as whimsical as love and sorrow
only in the ultimate consciousness
can one make it come and stay.
I have forgiven
a thousand times,
and reneged almost as many.
You see I believe it's only
my limitations that recall
the revenge.
You see I really believe
we are all born with forgiveness.
You see I have always
forgiven them

deep deep down.
I never ever really blamed them
Not even for one second.
In timeless truth
I believe they are just my teachers.
You see it is up to me
to learn patience, grace and
the dance that lets life
go and flow
with(in) the freedom of
forgiveness.
    —Sandra Monks

38

Thoughts on Letting Go

Teach us to care and not to care
Teach us to sit still
—T. S. Eliot

Finally, I knew I had to let go of Sandra. I had to look at the fact that, after fifty years, I could not help—and nine months of therapy together had not worked. I could not fix it and neither could anyone else. Some twenty-five years of working with Jerome, trying to understand how to help Sandra and exploring my past went by the wayside when Sandra started drinking.

The anger I began feeling at her destruction of others and of herself became something I couldn't control. Sometimes I wanted to tear my daughter to pieces and sometimes I wanted to hold her in my arms. But neither was possible. I am not sure there is any greater failure than the failure to help your child. As Sandra kept saying, "You brought me here." If your child has cancer or another physical disease, you can reach out and be with her—comfort her. With mental illness, it is often not so.

Reading a book called *This Stranger My Son* helped. Written by Louise Wilson in 1968, it is the harrowing story of a family trying to come to terms with their tragically mentally ill son. His rages became frightening and the financial toll mounted up as they had other children to support. The mother was an artist and gave it up. They finally found a home for their son with a psychiatrist who also took in others. The mother wrote at the end of the book:

*This, then, is the chronicle of our family up till now.
This is as far as I can go. I ask myself why I have told
the story at all, and the answer is: because from time
to time in every life there comes a need to sort out long
thoughts. I had to know where we stood and how this
family of six human beings might have been changed
by its experiences.*

*If in any small way our story can relieve other
families, other parents, who have been carrying the
same fearful burden, it will have been worth telling.
I believe it can do so, even if it does no more than say:
You are not alone. I know I gained strength when I
learned my child was only one of thousands who had
dropped silently out of sight. It gave me courage to see
that so many others were enduring the same affliction
with so much courage.*

It had been three years since this mother had seen her
son or talked with him. She understood that she might not
see him for years. "There are no more mirages for us—the
sickness is there, that's all—for now anyway," however much
they love him. At the very end of the book, she goes to the
attic and gets out her easel, and claims back her life.

I am not sure now I could ever completely let Sandra
go. We both live on the island, not quite a mile apart. We
always hear things from family and friends. The telephone
calls never stopped, drunk and often vicious and cruel calls
to members of the family, devastating, making the kind
of remark one never forgets—close to the bone—and she
became physically intrusive as well. Eventually she called
the police so often—at least three hundred times—that
criminal charges were filed, which in court would mean
two years in jail.

Psychic intrusion was a large part of what was so frightening for me. I once mentioned to Jerome that at times I felt

psychically invaded by Sandra with anger that didn't belong to me or suicidal thoughts that weren't mine. Jerome was quiet for a minute and then said that Sandra's illness can sometimes make her act like a psychic terrorist. This was discovered at McLean when she was there. Jerome said that those around such people, including some psychiatrists, feel as if they are going crazy too. Those with a borderline personality can invade one's mind with their reality and eat away at others. Some psychiatrists have caught themselves thinking like their patients, or feeling as if their own personalities were endangered and feeling obligated to behave the way the patients want them to. When Jerome paused, I asked if this happened because Sandra wanted to hurt me or if she was very upset and angry about something. He said it was more like a force that she couldn't control. I was very relieved that I had come to recognize this and could guard against it, for both our sakes—Sandra's and mine. In a way, I suppose freeing myself of a psychic invasion is a way of letting go, but I have to ask myself: *Have I really? Is one able to let go of someone they love so much?*

One day Bobby and I were stunned to see an article, accompanied by a photograph of Sandra, on the front page of our local Sunday city paper. She was quoted as having said, among other things, that she had been arrested many times for public drunkenness and finally received a year-and-a-half jail sentence and had lost custody of her daughter. But because of a new device, an ankle bracelet that immediately let the police know if she'd been drinking, she had not been drinking for over a year, which was quite an accomplishment. She'd even started to sing again.

39

Jerome and Healing

I have dreamed and half dreamed this book into existence—often dreaming backwards. I could not have written it faster than I could have dreamed it and until the psyche released it. I can leave it now to blow away with the clouds. —My notes

Shortly after I wrote in my journal about letting Sandra go, I was again sitting in Jerome's office in Santa Fe. There was a small log fire burning. I didn't say anything for a while, then I said that I wanted to talk about what Sandra had scratched on the wall of her solitary confinement cell: "I am me and I have a right to be."

"I could have scratched that on the wall of my childhood bedroom behind the locked door." I paused and took a deep breath and asked, "Could I have passed that feeling on to Sandra because of my mother?"

I continued without pausing for an answer that I did not want to hear. I told Jerome that I don't really understand the psychic connection between a mother and a daughter, especially if they are both intuitive and fairly psychic, but I believe it exists and is very strong (with all children and mothers).

After my break with Sandra, Bobby and I went to Northern Island in the fall as usual and had some time alone there. The morning after we arrived—as the first ray of light slanted over the black water on the bay—the bull started to bellow, sounding like all the world's agony in long, loud, thrusting, pitiful wails, piercing through the morning's immense stillness. There was no response from the cows, only the rooster had woken up and started his more cheerful song to greet the day. There were no birds yet; a herd of deer ran by, then across the field and toward the chapel in the woods.

I was in my swing overlooking the bay. It was about 5:30; the bull was at it again. A singer should take note—the breath controls the intensity of feeling, the whole body resonates. It was painful to listen and my own body began to respond and resonate uncomfortably. Finally someone brought the baton down and the chorus began together. The loons twittered and moaned, the crows cackled, and the other birds sang their songs; even the crickets started chirping, and soft wings flapped gently and floated over the hill, field, and bay.

But in the bull's persistence, I heard the Buddha's words—that life is *dukkha*, usually translated as "suffering." Or Albert Schweitzer's "Only at quite rare moments have I felt really glad to be alive—I could not but feel with a symphony full of regret all the pain that I saw around me not only of men but of the whole creation." And I wished the bull would stop. I went inside the house and turned on some Bach.

We found out late in the day it was not a bull but a cow that had just lost its child. Evidently the mom had a poor temperament, and the calf had become impossible to manage. The owners took the calf on the boat to the mainland to sell. Its mother bellowed in pain. Neither Bobby nor I could stop thinking about Sandra and ourselves.

Now, I told Jerome, I have to go back to what I thought intuitively, not really knowing it, as a child, and to what I have written painfully as an adult. I felt, in some way, my mother was telling me to die. I was full of poison and was an unwanted rape baby—I'm sure she didn't understand that—or to put it another way, I was not to be. I became a stranger in a strange world. So I became fascinated and attracted to the north wind, which represents death in George MacDonald's book, *At the Back of the North Wind*. I found in this beautiful, sparkling goddess, who sat in the frozen north on her throne of death, a mother. The north wind became my mother and teacher. How I loved her.

If my mother's message was death, I was going to seek it out. Bobby's godson, a young doctor in London, has Crohn's disease and officially died on the operating table and came back. He said death was the most beautiful thing that ever happened to him, like being picked up in the arms of his mother, and he would never be afraid of death again.

But there was the message from my mother not to be, not to be all that I could be—not to sing, not to know how to grow a skin, not to feel I belong here. I have to know, as a mother, did I pass that on to my daughter? I know she possesses her own feelings, ideas, and personality, but she has a beautiful voice and a love of singing. How much of the message, *Die*, did I pass on to her?

I told Jerome that I needed to know, too, if perhaps Sandra's response to my passing on such a message was, in some ways, healthy. It was outrage, anger, frustration, while mine was sorrow and constant mourning. Perhaps if I could have sung, I could have helped her, but I couldn't and didn't know why. Perhaps healing oneself is the best gift—sending a message, *Yes, it's all right to be.* How I wish for her to sing her song and write her book.

Jerome didn't say a word. He just listened. I had been on such a long journey with him. I took a breath, smiled through tears, and said that the spirits were kind to give me a guide in the form of a six-foot-six bearded Jungian analyst, who looks as if he just walked out of the desert with Moses. I thanked Jerome for helping me stay here in this strange place without boundaries, without feet placed firmly on the earth, without a skin; for helping me to grow boundaries, to look at the truth, to learn to be loved, to belong here, to create while here; and for reminding me, when overcome by a black energy or force, to try to keep a little light going in this world.

I started taking yoga classes. Through the encourage-ment of my Transcendental Meditation friends, I started meditating regularly again. I would feel tension melt away and begin to understand how one could prepare for a spiritual experience.

I understand that a mantra is a sacred sound-vibration that awakens and stimulates the intuitive qualities of the mind and the spirit and enables one to move into different stages of higher consciousness. My friends, who have meditated for many years, appear to be in a state of happiness or bliss. Are they closer to death? Maharishi replied yes to my question: "Is meditating a small death?" Have my friends moved away from the confines of the physical to the spiritual? Are their auras filled with light that resides in the silence and stillness? Are they very intuitive and psychic—do they move easily through the connectedness of things? Do they lose the boundary of the skin?

In my second year of chemotherapy for breast cancer, the doctor told me I could not continue with chemo, as my white blood cell count was too low—a serious situation. I asked him to let me try extra meditation—I was doing the flying and levitating sutras. For three weeks I meditated for about two hours in the morning and two in the evening, and it was something that made me happy. When I went back to the hospital, my white blood cell count was up and I continued with the chemo; the doctors were amazed.

Some two years after I visited Jerome, I got an invitation from Angus to go to Santa Fe together for a week. We stayed at a charming small hotel with an outdoor dining area. The days were warm and sunny, and there was a silence in the desert and small mountains surrounding the place. I loved to sit out on the terrace having breakfast and talking about a multitude of things with Angus, or finding a delightful restaurant for dinner and wandering through the streets exploring the town. It was a magical time.

40

Song

Everything temporal is a metaphor
Everything eternal is but a metaphor
—Unknown

To be a metaphor and grow a skin is an odd task. Once one has a skin, one's image will appear in the mirror. A metaphor does not have a reflection. I am told, or am able to hear now and then, that my image has been or is sometimes beautiful, and I look in the mirror and smile, glad someone sees beauty there—I see an elderly lady with wrinkles, but I hope perhaps what they see is what Jerome told me the Navajo medicine men and community say when they heal someone who has been ill: "They walk in beauty—in health." After the healing ceremonies, the word *beauty* is chanted again and again.

> *The world before me is restored in beauty*
> *The world behind me is restored in beauty*
> *The world below me is restored in beauty*
> *The world above me is restored in beauty*
> *All things around me are restored in beauty*
> *My voice is restored in beauty*
> *It is finished in beauty*
> *It is finished in beauty*
> *It is finished in beauty*
> *It is finished in beauty*

I took Sidra for a singing lesson when she was seventeen, as I wanted her to be familiar with the idea of having singing lessons with a good teacher, if she ever wanted them. She has a lovely voice. Some years later she was to become a professional singer. Afterward, I asked if I could take some lessons too.

As I walked in for my first lesson at the age of seventy-two, the myth of Orpheus ran through my mind, and I could see myself, many years ago, standing beside our Cambridge neighbor Eric Schroeder and hearing him say, "You will not sing—a few concerts, that's all."

The first, second, and third lessons were mostly about breathing. In the second lesson, something snapped open and I started to breathe deeply. I felt as if I'd never taken a deep breath before—as if the skin on my lower body moved and I floated in my skin and stretched against the breath. Something released, and I controlled it. I believe that before then I had been in a fight-or-flight mode, with short, shallow breaths that would end up strangling and tightening the jaw and throat until the heart, afraid to feel, would stop the breath. One cannot sing that way.

By the third lesson, I was singing *Carmen*. I could have sustained the high notes better, but I felt I had probably never sung so well. "Look in the mirror," my teacher said. Looking at her and then in the mirror, I could see my reflection and copy her. I was amazed; I think she was too. It is impossible to sing when breathing in a fight-or-flight mode—when the heart isn't free to express feelings, and the throat closes, there is no support, and without support there is no voice.

We had to leave for London for quite a long time after that, and I have not been back yet. I so hope that my voice will still be there, and, if it is, that I will sing again.

41

Skin and Love

Body hurt but flying—everyone's scandalous flaw is mine.
—Rumi

I wrote that letting go would have other connotations as life moved on, and it has been both painful and rewarding. Letting go of the fear of knowing about oneself—the part one would rather not deal with—requires one to understand what effect one's psyche and unconscious life can have on others and the powerful need to protect oneself from knowing.

It is known that babies that are not held in the first years of their lives often die or become psychotic when they grow into childhood. I wonder, on hearing that, what does it have to do with love? When one is touched, does love melt through the skin to the heart and through the eyes by being seen, even through the taste of milk, through the sense of smell and even through the sounds heard in the lullaby of the voice? Is love like lighting a candle and passing on light—is that what keeps us here? Without feeling loved or touched, and often living with fear, the sense of self that should be assured by the surrounding skin instead begins to feel like it's evaporating—the lines of the body disappearing—so that the child dies or grows up with wounds. Perhaps that is why or how some people become psychic; they have had nothing to attach to or with. The mind gains a sense of structure by telling the body what to do, but people who can't achieve this state often feel confused and disorganized, and their hearts feel crushed or lonely. The terrible and exhausting fight begins against the discovery that one isn't loved, and there is shame in that.

For the rest of my life I suspect I will need to be alone a lot, and I have a habit of disappearing if around people too long. I still get exhausted by the way I take things in, as if I am porous. I've needed to learn how to protect myself. I need to recover and digest impressions around me. Learning to be alone is a gift in a way. Although to this day if I am left alone at night, I lock up the house and head quickly up the stairs to my room. But not before I catch a glimpse of a shadow standing behind a curtain, or someone sitting in the dark in a chair dead still. When I reach my room, I slam our large brass locks shut and whisper, "I'm sorry, I'm so sorry." I don't know why.

The fear of an empty house (not of being alone) only gets worse as I get older. But the worst fear, almost terror, is of being loved, and if love leaks into the heart, the reaction is a slight pain, salt water covering the eyes, and a feeling of alarm, like a small animal about to be attacked—a stranger in a strange world. But I am learning to set my own boundaries now. I feel, as the French say, *mieux dans ma peau*—I am more comfortable in my skin.

In my need for a mother the north wind became my mother; my sparkling Goddess who sat on her throne of death or carried me above the world, over the sea, rivers, fields – instructing me in life's secrets – some so difficult – but in her arms, I could hear them. How it was when she caused the sailors to drown, that she could hear the most beautiful music and she knew it was alright – and I could hear the music too. I had, for me, the most powerful, dangerous, loving mother and dancing mother – how I love and fear her.

The winds swirl and push around my head whispering, coaxing, "We will carry you away – spread your wings out." It is then I hear the flapping of soft wings around my ears and know the morning dove is settling in my heart; wild creature, singing in the green, wet, whirling leaves of my brain and whispering of light and death.

I have earned my skin—my place here—but I can still fly and dance through the connectedness of things, still be a metaphor and live close to the spirit. There is a saying: "The sage whose senses, mind, and intellect are controlled (through meditating) is liberated from desire, fear, and anger, is indeed forever free, and lives in a state of bliss/ happiness."

42

Old Age and the Life of the Spirit

Death is just a resting place
On the path of evolution.
If one understood correctly—one would cry
at birth and celebrate at death.
—The Maharishi Mahesh Yogi

I don't remember when it was that I realized I was old. The face and the body disintegrate so gently that one accommodates oneself to it without realizing something in life has changed—entered a new phase. I think I am between acceptance and rebellion, the body sometimes having the last word. I have learned to accept the deaths of friends and family—not without sorrow; exploring ideas, writing; I will sing and dance a bit, and perhaps will pull some of the old company dancers together and do a group of healing dances, using tai chi and shamanic drumming. (I have been told I can heal, which reminds me of being touched and told this by a healer years ago.)

I think often now of being seventy-five and, half-dreaming in the morning, of how much time is left, and I add it up on my fingers while half-asleep. It could be years or less or many more. Sometimes there are moments of slight fear. They pass, but I am aware of the strangeness of being here again, and the slight sorrow and pain I will probably always feel—the sadness that forms around my heart like a thin layer of ice, but often when I meditate, my gentle Ping Pong watches and my fierce little shih tzu, Shiva, jumps into the cradle of my crossed legs and sighs, and while I meditate, I believe I hear a cracking of the ice as it melts away.

In the early morning I push myself up, arms on my pillows, and look out the large glass sliding doors on the second floor, which open onto a good-size porch in the shape of a boat's bow. Below there is nothing but the ocean, closer lately and breaking about twenty yards away, and I feel as if I were floating through quiet seas or rocking through rolling waves. Sometimes I see a gray day and a dark gray ocean, but far away on the horizon there is a brilliant ribbon of silver light between the horizon and the sea. When I sit in my study, which feels to me like a slightly swaying tower, later in the day, I watch the incoming tide push relentlessly up the curved white beach. There is fierceness in the ocean, a swelling that I don't remember from before. Long fingers of white foam crash from the curve of roaring waves and pour their way up to the dunes as if reaching for them. Then as the tide recedes, it pulls further and further away, leaving a broader expanse of beach than I have ever seen. My tower rocks over sparkling swells and waves.

Why these salt tears?

Sometimes I feel the world is tilting, and I wonder if it will tilt too far (or am I the one that is tilting?)—have we slowly destroyed it? There is an imbalance of female and male energy; the female doesn't know her real power yet. Why have we never explored or studied why men go to war? Why are religions at war again and again?

There are those with greater vision than I who say it's all perfect. Many of them are having extraordinary experiences while meditating, and people are meditating around the world now. I believe some five million T.M. mediators.

Yet, no matter how much we—women in particular— exercise the body, nourish it properly, and take medicine for stress, we often we feel depleted. How odd it is that we don't exercise the other half of our human condition, the spirit, through yoga and meditation or prayer, and seek spiritual knowledge, when by so doing we could balance ourselves with both intuition and intellect.

Researchers at M.I.T. have studied the Dalai Lama's brain and found that in the area where happiness lies, his brain is larger—and he claims to be happy. I believe he achieves this state through certain ancient sounds, meditations, and concepts. I am sure prayer is powerful, too; I pray every day after my meditation for guidance and healing for others.

I find now, when meditating, a tremendous physical and mental peace comes over me. I am beginning to see "visions"—I don't know what you'd call them—like dreams a bit, only clearer and occurring while wide-awake and meditating. I don't know how to translate or explain them. My friends who have meditated for a long time say it is seeing with the eye of God—symbolized in the place where Indians put the red mark on their foreheads. My meditating friends are seeing extraordinary things. Through meditation they are discovering we can actually change the brain now—but is there time? For those who meditate and pray, I believe eventually there comes "the peace that passeth all understanding."

43

Shifts

Now, in 2008, scientists have discovered the following information and for the first time, there is real hope out there for borderline patients; although it may take some time, it's an incredible breakthrough and will alleviate so much suffering.

Below is a summary of some information I received in June of 2008:[3]

Scientists Identify Brain Abnormalities Underlying Key Element of Borderline Personality Disorder

Using new approaches, an interdisciplinary team of scientists at NewYork-Presbyterian Hospital/ Weill Cornell Medical Center in New York City has gained a view of activity in key brain areas associated with a core difficulty in patients with borderline personality disorder—shedding new light on this serious psychiatric condition.

"In this study, our collaborative team looked specifically at the nexus between negative emotions and impulsivity—the tendency of people with borderline personality disorder to 'act out' destructively in the presence of anger," Dr. Silbersweig explains.

---

[3] The article is reproduced in full at the back of the book in the appendix. Reproduced with permission from www.medicalnewstoday.com.

"Previous work by our group and others had suggested that an area at the base of the brain within the ventromedial prefrontal cortex was key to people's ability to restrain behaviors in the presence of emotion," Dr. Silbersweig continues.

"The more that this type of work gets done, the more people will understand that mental illness is not the patient's fault—that there are circuits in the brain that control these functions in humans and that these disorders are tied to fundamental disruptions in these circuits," Dr. Silbersweig says. "Our hope is that such insights will help erode the stigma surrounding psychiatric illness."

The new discovery creates a shift in my mind. So much of the guilt I sustained came from feeling I might be the cause and from trying to discover how and why, so I could change and change the situation and, if possible, reach Sandra in some way. I begin to feel that Bobby and especially myself weren't the cause of so much anger and pain—though I still feel as a mother, perhaps there was more I could have done, and the shift in my mind is slow. It's been fifty years but I still hear Sandra saying, "The final snag in the defeating battle was the rage that would well up and take me over." I am still in the jail where the tormentor comes out of the dark and joins us at poker—no one wins. But now I leave the poker table and walk toward a gate, which I find open. I stand there and I hear whispers from the blackness softly calling out "shame shame." I cannot walk through it—not yet.

44

Family and the Reverend

Fifty years. It has been an adventure – a funny, furious, risky, loving, sad, beautiful adventure. I wouldn't have it any other way and I intend to follow and enfold you for at least the next two millenniums.

It will be easy—when we are between "takes" here. I'll look around the Universe and the stars and planets and see this great ball of energy sparkling and dancing this way and that and then take straight off like a shooting star and I'll recognize you, my tall, blue-eyed Irish man, and I'll just hurry along to catch up or maybe I'll beckon. One way or another I'll always find you because that's where I belong. With all my love, always, always.

—Sent from me to Bobby on our fiftieth wedding anniversary

In so many ways I have been extraordinarily fortunate— three incredible islands in my life have held and enfolded me, and now on Crescent Island I have some sixty relatives living here, some permanent, some come and go—a family community. We have funds to pay for our health and our families' and to live comfortably by the sea.

I am blessed to have our son and daughter-in-law, Emma, and our grandchildren living next door. It is a constant source of joy, comfort, and fun watching Angus and Emma bring up their children with so much love and guidance, and watching them thrive and having the privilege of being included has been part of the happiest time of my life. Emma is very beautiful, intelligent, loving and fun, and is now a child advocate whom I love dearly as a friend as well as a daughter-in-law. Angus has made his mark on the world running a huge corporation and has a strong interest in politics. Sidra is eighteen now and we have had many wonderful times together and some sad and serious talks. I so want her to be happy and productive, but I do worry terribly.

It is quite an incredible and magnificent thing to have a community of family in this day and age—a place to go home to. We even have a few Democrats!

I have become an Interfaith Minister so I am now the Reverend Milly. I can marry people, bury them, and perhaps raise them up—somehow. What I hope to do is write my thoughts and explore matters of the spirit, religion, and science and along the way, if I can be of some comfort to others and help some to remember to laugh—and explore—that would be good.

Now, in old age, it sometimes feels like sipping morphine tea, if there is such a thing. Perhaps it comes with the calming of emotions and the constant reminder we and our friends are moving on. That is a different perspective from which to view life. It is perhaps the final letting go. Life seems like a pause between two worlds, but the "other" world seems closer, the world of the spirit gives its comfort and reminders more readily—for which I am grateful.

Now, as in the Vedic tradition and in the phases of my three islands, there is youth and the mother, then family work and the father, and in the last phase the elders go to the forest to practice the spiritual life as that is where they will be going. I am looking forward now to exploring the spiritual life—exploring the concept of light—perhaps also exploring the dance world again, writing, family, friends, and being with Bobby. Bobby speaks all over the world on governance issues—keeps starting new businesses and new adventures of the mind and writing. We have our puppies—who often sit at our feet until they are picked up and held—warm, furry bundles. Shiva is a true little god of dance and destruction and sometimes when I hold him, I hear him growl gently. Bobby says he is purring but I don't think so. I know I am holding the god of destruction in my arms but it's all right. When I hold him next to my heart I remember that's where love resides too. They say the heart gives off much more energy than the mind or brain, which is the intellect, and the heart is intuitive and that's where intuition lies, and maybe consciousness.

Now I sit in my tower overlooking the sea on this wet and very windy spring day—we have six rocking chairs on our porch facing the ocean. Whenever the wind blows, they rock back and forth as if some restless spirit settled in them rocking and laughing wildly and I am tempted to go down and ask them, what is so funny? Is it all just some kind of odd joke after all? But I let them rock—I'm not sure I want to know.

In the spring here it is an enchanted time, as many birds are in flight and singing. I think we are nearer to angels then than at any other time of year. If the angels won't come and fold me in their warm, tickling feathered wings, as I have been praying and asking them to, I still have the birds to soar and sing with until my north wind returns.

45

Northern Island—Final

The one light appears in diverse forms.
—The Bhagavad-Gita

Our boat slid quietly across the ocean in the still autumn air toward Northern Island, which took shape in front of us. As we docked and walked up in the field, the land smelled of growing things drying up, the smell of death and sleep mixed with the sweet smell of pine; nothing moved, not the trees or grasses. The birds had disappeared. There was no sound except the humming of autumn. We slept well that night.

The next day before dawn I sat in my hammock and thought of the three islands and all the stories they held—of all the islands, this one was the most peaceful.

Later that afternoon Bobby and I walked to the chapel on the path, with its thick roots and brown pine needles over spongy, light-green moss, and through the straight, towering trunks of the cathedral pines. The light sifting through them made it more beautiful than any cathedral.

We ended our walk by making our way slowly up the hill to the new graveyard that has an opening facing the bay. The coming evening was clear and softly lit. On our arrival, we bowed our heads and stood by the grave of our much-loved brother-in-law, the first occupant, and then we turned and sat on the stone wall overlooking the bay. Sitting here, we knew that whatever our lives had been, we were grateful to have participated, to have been here together and to have loved each other, and we knew that we would be buried here. I smiled at Bobby. "We are whirling in space, take my hand." He took my hand.

In the early evening, the birds spread their wings without singing and the gulls floated on their silent journey home. The fields across the bay caught God's backlighting and it spread across them like flames of soft purple and orange. The crescent moon rose, carrying its shadow in the curve of its arms. The shooting stars soon blazed against the gathering darkness; there was a moment of stillness—the waves silently folded over and over as we sat there on that gently rocking island.

Acknowledgments

To my husband, Bobby, I am so thankful we have been together in this circle of time, and for all your help—always—that made our islands float comfortably into words and kept the ocean tides and storms from battering them, so their songs could be heard.

To Sandra, with gratitude for reading *Songs of Three Islands* and letting me know how you felt about some of it—you felt parts of it were inaccurate or taken out of context and that might be hurtful to others—I can appreciate that and so, my special thanks for writing, "It is your book and your memories and perspective—hope you take this in good faith."

How can I thank Lee Hope, my editor and friend, who made this book possible? It started about eight years ago at the Stonecoast program Lee was running for the University of Southern Maine. I took my first course with Michael Steinberg. I found him a most extraordinary teacher. I went to Stonecoast three more times and was quietly encouraged to keep writing my book. Lee ran two more programs for writers, which I also went to, one at Pine Manor in Massachusetts and the other at Eckerd College in Florida. In time, she found me Tanya Whiton, a young writer who had the thankless job of organizing the book in linear time—not circular, in which I am more comfortable—and she really had a bit of a struggle, aside from making many valuable observations about flights of fancy that the reader might not understand. She was a great help.

Lee, with persistence, patience, and kindness, kept letting me know she believed the book was worth writing. I began to believe maybe the book deserved an editor, and worked up my courage to ask her if she would edit it—not an easy task, as the book rushed in many directions. The subject matter could sometimes be very delicate, and her thoughtfulness and expertise were amazing to me. So, I thank Lee Hope for starting my Three Islands on an adventure they would not have had otherwise.

My thanks to Al Alvarez for his encouragement when I sent him the beginning of this book—as he is a well-known writer, his words meant a great deal to me.

My thanks to Peggy Alexander at Wiley, who kept encouraging me; she was a great incentive to go on with it.

Thanks to Sandra Hochman, whom my friend Dale Coudert introduced me to on our time in Florida during winter months. Sandra ran a group of writers (over several years)—all women, all in our late sixties, whose memoirs were powerful, sad, insightful, and just plain extraordinary.

To Chris DeSantis, who took care of all the many, many things that kept our place functioning so I could write.

My thanks to James Atlas for his thoughtful and very helpful work in making this a more comprehensive and just a plain better book. It was a great pleasure working with him and a learning experience; I am grateful knowing the book is more than it would have been without his help.

And a special thank-you to Lisa Johnson, who, over four years, typed and retyped, organized, never complained, and, thank heavens, corrected my spelling, but most of all had the kindness and tact never to make a comment about many things in the book that were painful. I am truly grateful for her wise and helpful nature.

I would like to thank Terence Guardino in Palm Springs, my astrologer for some twenty years. His encouragement and help in difficult times have meant a great deal to me.

For almost thirty years now, Jerome S. Bernstein, Jungian analyst, has been my guide, sometimes through the underworld and sometimes through the amazing truth of dreams, sometimes providing just comfort, and sometimes untangling differences and for me and our family—for all the many awakenings, the understanding and care given to us—is a simple thanks enough? Perhaps it's best to try to live a life with understanding, compassion, intelligence, creativity, and of course love.

Appendix I

The following article appeared on the website MedicalNews-Today.com.

Scientists Identify Brain Abnormalities Underlying Key Element of Borderline Personality Disorder

December 21, 2007

Using new approaches, an interdisciplinary team of scientists at New York-Presbyterian Hospital/Weill Cornell Medical Center in New York City has gained a view of activity in key brain areas associated with a core difficulty in patients with borderline personality disorder—shedding new light on this serious psychiatric condition.

"It's early days yet, but the work is pinpointing functional differences in the neurobiology of healthy people versus individuals with the disorder as they attempt to control their behavior in a negative emotional context. Such initial insights can help provide a foundation for better, more targeted therapies down the line," explains lead researcher Dr. David A. Silbersweig, the Stephen P. Tobin and Dr. Arnold M. Cooper Professor of Psychiatry and Professor of Neurology at Weill Cornell Medical College, and attending psychiatrist and neurologist at NewYork-Presbyterian Hospital/Weill Cornell Medical Center.

The findings are featured in this month's issue of the

American Journal of Psychiatry.

Borderline personality disorder is a devastating mental illness that affects between 1 and 2 percent of Americans, causing untold disruption of patients' lives and relationships. Nevertheless, its underlying biology is not very well understood. Hallmarks of the illness include impulsivity, emotional instability, interpersonal difficulties, and a preponderance of negative emotions such as anger—all of which may encourage or be associated with substance abuse, self-destructive behaviors and even suicide.

"In this study, our collaborative team looked specifically at the nexus between negative emotions and impulsivity— the tendency of people with borderline personality disorder to 'act out' destructively in the presence of anger," Dr. Silbersweig explains. "Other studies have looked at either negative emotional states or this type of behavioral disinhibition. The two are closely connected, and we wanted to find out why. We therefore focused our experiments on the interaction between negative emotional states and behavioral inhibition."

Advanced brain-scanning technologies developed by the research team made it possible to detect the brain areas of interest with greater sensitivity.

"Previous work by our group and others had suggested that an area at the base of the brain within the ventromedial prefrontal cortex was key to people's ability to restrain behaviors in the presence of emotion," Dr. Silbersweig explains.

Unfortunately, tracking activity in this brain region has been extremely difficult using functional MRI (fMRI). "Due to its particular location, you get a lot of signal loss," the researcher explains.

However, the Weill Cornell team used a special fMRI activation probe that they developed to eliminate much of that interference. This paved the way for the study, which included 16 patients with borderline personality disorder and 14 healthy controls.

The team also used a tailored fMRI neuropsychological approach to observe activity in the subjects' ventromedial prefrontal cortex as they performed what behavioral neuroscience researchers call "go/no go" tests.

These rapid-fire tests require participants to press or withhold from pressing a button whenever they receive particular visual cues. In a twist from the usual approach, the performance of the task with negative words (related to borderline psychology) was contrasted with the performance of the task when using neutral words, to reveal how negative emotions affect the participants' ability to perform the task.

As expected, negative emotional words caused participants with borderline personality disorder to have more difficulty with the task at hand and act more impulsively—ignoring visual cues to stop as they repeatedly pressed the button.

But what was really interesting was what showed up on the fMRI.

"We confirmed that discrete parts of the ventromedial prefrontal cortex—the subgenual anterior cingulate cortex and the medial orbitofrontal cortex areas—were relatively less active in patients versus controls," Dr. Silbersweig says. "These areas are thought to be key to facilitating behavioral inhibition under emotional circumstances, so if they are underperforming that could contribute to the disinhibition one so often sees with borderline personality disorder."

At the same time, the research team observed heightened levels of activation during the tests in other areas of the patients' brains, including the amygdala, a locus for emotions such as anger and fear, and some of the brain's other limbic regions, which are linked to emotional processing.

"In the frontal region and the amygdala, the degree to which the brain aberrations occurred was closely correlated to the degree with which patients with borderline personality disorder had clinical difficulty controlling their behavior, or had difficulty with negative emotion, respectively," Dr. Silbersweig notes.

The study sheds light not only on borderline personality disorder, but on the mechanisms healthy individuals rely on to curb their tempers in the face of strong emotion.

Still, patients struggling with borderline personality disorder stand to benefit most from this groundbreaking research. An accompanying journal commentary labels the study "rigorous" and "systematic," and one of the first to validate with neuroimaging what scientists had only been able to guess at before.

"The more that this type of work gets done, the more people will understand that mental illness is not the patient's fault—that there are circuits in the brain that control these functions in humans and that these disorders are tied to fundamental disruptions in these circuits," Dr. Silbersweig says. "Our hope is that such insights will help erode the stigma surrounding psychiatric illness."

The research could even help lead to better treatment.

As pointed out in the commentary, the research may help explain how specific biological or psychological therapies could ease symptoms of borderline personality disorder for some patients, by addressing the underlying biology of impulsivity in the context of overwhelming negative emotion. The more scientists understand the neurological aberrations that give rise to the disorder, the greater the hope for new, highly targeted drugs or other therapeutic interventions.

"Going forward, we plan to test hypotheses about changes in these brain regions associated with various types of treatment," Dr. Silbersweig says. "Such work by ourselves and others could help confirm these initial findings and point the way to better therapies."

This work was funded by the Borderline Personality Disorder Research Foundation and the DeWitt Wallace

Fund of the New York Community Trust.

Co-researchers include senior author Dr. Emily Stern, as well as Dr. John F. Clarkin, Dr. Martin Goldstein, Dr. Otto F. Kernberg, Dr. Oliver Tuescher, Dr. Kenneth N. Levy, Dr. Gary Brendel, Dr. Hong Pan, Dr. Manfred Beutel, Dr. Jane Epstein, Dr. Mark F. Lenzenweger, Dr. Kathleen M. Thomas, Dr. Michael I. Posner, and Michelle T. Pavony—all of NewYork-Presbyterian Hospital/Weill Cornell Medical Center.

Appendix II

The following is a transcription of the letter from Andrew Carnegie that appears on pages 15-17.

Andrew Carnegie
New York May 8th, '76

I cannot allow this foundation day of second furnace to pass unnoticed. It has given me the greatest satisfaction received from business for some years. We are now on the right road to bring our investments down to permanent value. "Founded on the rock" we shall be - our course to a pre eminent position among the Iron Groups of America – yes of the world – seems very clear to me.

We need only apply our profits to the development of our business, even undertaking an extension for which we have not the means.

I shall endeavor to restrain my natural tendency to go at a rapid pace. You will agree to move as we earn the means always, however in development on improvement of the iron and steel builders and not outside thereof–and never let us have notes out exceeding a small sum for months. I agree to this will all my heart–and am content to make less rather than to give cause for the least anxiety–saying "to be thus is nothing but to be safely thus".

We must remember however that we are too

young not to grow and it is only a question whether we concentrate, or scatter our means. For my part I would have the young Carnegie and Phipps succeed at some great interest in which their pride can be surely enlisted and to a vast establishment which will necessarily require their close attention, otherwise I could scarcely blame my nephews were they to turn aside into no bodies—or worse.

The satisfaction I have in feeling that our firm consists of you alone is unbounded. How happily we are placed and how well calculated to supplement each other (except that I always feel my money is necessary to fire me) equal part in the credit as it is to your services most is owing.

Three cheers for "Lucy No 2" and hurrah for O B Y C.

Yours
The Senior